D1462176

Contending *for* OUR ALL

BOOKS BY JOHN PIPER

God's Passion for His Glory
The Pleasures of God
Desiring God
The Dangerous Duty of Delight
Future Grace
A Hunger for God
Let the Nations Be Glad!
A Godward Life
Pierced by the Word
Seeing and Savoring Jesus Christ
The Legacy of Sovereign Joy
The Hidden Smile of God
The Roots of Endurance
The Misery of Job and the Mercy of God
The Innkeeper
The Prodigal's Sister
Recovering Biblical Manhood and Womanhood
What's the Difference?
The Justification of God
Counted Righteous in Christ
Brothers, We Are Not Professionals
The Supremacy of God in Preaching
Beyond the Bounds
Don't Waste Your Life
The Passion of Jesus Christ
Life as a Vapor
A God-Entranced Vision of All Things
When I Don't Desire God
Sex and the Supremacy of Christ
Taste and See
God Is the Gospel

the swans are not silent

BOOK FOUR

Contending
for OUR ALL

Defending Truth and Treasuring Christ
in the Lives of Athanasius, John Owen,
and J. Gresham Machen

JOHN PIPER

CROSSWAY BOOKS

A PUBLISHING MINISTRY OF
GOOD NEWS PUBLISHERS
WHEATON, ILLINOIS

Cover design: James Benn

Cover photo: Getty Images

First printing, 2006

Printed in the United States of America

Library of Congress Cataloging-in-Publication Data
Piper, John, 1946-
  Contending for our all : defending truth and treasuring Christ in the lives of Athanasius, John Owen, and J. Gresham Machen / John Piper.
    p. cm. — (The swans are not silent ; bk. 4)
  Includes indexes.
  ISBN 13: 978-1-58134-676-3
  ISBN 10: 1-58134-676-X (hc : alk. paper)
    1. Athanasius, Saint, Patriarch of Alexandria, d. 373. 2. Owen, John, 1616-1683. 3. Machen, J. Gresham (John Gresham), 1881-1937. 4. Theologians—Biography. I. Title. II. Series.
BR1700.3.P55   2006
270.092'2—dc22   2005029262

QM		16	15	14	13	12	11	10	09	08	07	06
15	14	13	12	11	10	9	8	7	6	5	4	3	2	1

To
R. C. Sproul

Faithful Contender
for the Supreme Greatness of
the Holiness of God

CONTENTS

Our upbringing and the whole atmosphere of the world we live in make it certain that our main temptation will be that of yielding to winds of doctrine, not that of ignoring them. We are not at all likely to be hidebound: we are very likely indeed to be the slaves of fashion. If one has to choose between reading the new books and reading the old, one must choose the old: not because they are necessarily better but because they contain precisely those truths of which our own age is neglectful. The standard of permanent Christianity must be kept clear in our minds and it is against that standard that we must test all contemporary thought.

In fact, we must at all costs not *move with the times.*

We serve One who said, "Heaven and Earth shall move with the times, but my words shall not move with the times"

(Matthew 24:35; Mark 13:31; Luke 21:33).

C. S. LEWIS, "CHRISTIAN APOLOGETICS," IN: ESSAY COLLECTION AND OTHER SHORT PIECES (LONDON: HARPERCOLLINS, 2000), P. 149

PREFACE

The title of this series of books, "The Swans Are Not Silent," comes from a story about St. Augustine. When he handed over his duties as the bishop of Hippo in North Africa in A.D. 326, his humble replacement, Eraclius, rose to speak and said, "The cricket chirps, the swan is silent."[1] Therefore, in titling this series "The Swans Are *Not* Silent" I mean to say that great voices like Augustine's have been heard all through church history, and we will do well to listen.

I am deeply thankful to God that the swans are not silent, and that the list of faith-inspiring heroes in Hebrews 11 did not end with the New Testament. God has worked through the lives of countless saints of whom we should say, "Though they died, they still speak" (cf. Hebrews 11:4).

Some swans are alive and sing in our own day. But not many. And only time will tell if their song will survive the centuries. But time has already rendered that judgment for hundreds of swans. They have died, and their work has stood the test of time. Their song is, therefore, especially valuable for us to hear. You can hear them by studying what they wrote and by reading good biographies about them. This use of your time is probably wiser than staying up-to-date with news that will be forgotten in a fortnight and with ideas that will prove powerless in ten years.

I know of no one who has made a case for the old authors and the old books better than C. S. Lewis (1898-1963). When he

---

[1] Peter Brown, *Augustine of Hippo* (Berkeley: University of California Press, 1969), p. 408.

neared sixty he confessed with humility and wisdom: "I have lived nearly sixty years with myself and my own century and am not so enamored of either as to desire no glimpse of a world beyond them."[2] The "world beyond them" was not future or make-believe. It was the world of the past.

He practiced what he preached by writing an introduction for Athanasius's *The Incarnation of the Word of God*, written probably in A.D. 318. At the risk of tempting you to put down the book in your hands and read only old books, I will nevertheless tell you what Lewis said about the reading of old books like the classic by Athanasius.

> There is a strange idea abroad that in every subject the ancient books should be read only by the professionals, and that the amateur should content himself with the modern books. . . . [Students are directed not to Plato but to books on Plato]— all about 'isms' and influences and only once in twelve pages telling him what Plato actually said. . . . But if he only knew, the great man, just because of his greatness, is much more intelligible than his modern commentator. . . .
>
> Now this seems to me topsy-turvy. Naturally, since I myself am a writer, I do not wish the ordinary reader to read no modern books. But if he must read only the new or only the old, I would advise him to read the old. And I would give him this advice precisely because he is an amateur and therefore much less protected than the expert against the dangers of an exclusive contemporary diet. A new book is still on its trial and the amateur is not in a position to judge it. It has to be tested against the great body of Christian thought down the ages, and all its hidden implications (often unsuspected by the author himself) have to be brought to light. . . .

[2] From C. S. Lewis, *Studies in Medieval and Renaissance Literature*, quoted in *The Quotable Lewis*, ed. Jerry Root and Wayne Martindale (Wheaton, IL: Tyndale House, 1989), p. 509.

It is a good rule, after reading a new book, never to allow yourself another new one till you have read an old one in between. If that is too much for you, you should at least read one old one to every three new ones. . . .

We all, therefore, need the books that will correct the characteristic mistakes of our own period. And that means the old books. . . . We may be sure that the characteristic blindness of the twentieth century—the blindness about which posterity will ask, "But how *could* they have thought that?"—lies where we have never suspected it, and concerns something about which there is untroubled agreement between Hitler and President Roosevelt or between Mr. H. G. Wells and Karl Barth. None of us can fully escape this blindness. . . . The only palliative is to keep the clean sea breeze of the centuries blowing through our minds, and this can be done only by reading old books.[3]

In this book I invite you to feel the "clean sea breeze" blowing from the fourth, seventeenth, and early twentieth centuries. Perhaps this will lure you to read what Athanasius, John Owen, and J. Gresham Machen wrote. Their lives are not only pleasant as refreshing breezes from distant times but are also needed as exemplary contenders for the purity and preciousness of biblical truth. I will try to explain why in the Introduction. For now I thank God again that these three swans are not silent and that they were willing to suffer for the sake of safeguarding the gospel for us. They would have all said with Athanasius, "We are contending for our all."[4]

---

[3] Now printed as C. S. Lewis, "On The Reading of Old Books," in *C. S. Lewis: Essay Collection and Other Short Pieces*, ed. Lesley Walmsley (London: HarperCollins, 2000), pp. 438-440.

[4] "Wherefore . . . considering that *this struggle is for our all* . . . let us also make it our earnest care and aim to guard what we have received." *Athanasius: Select Works and Letters*, in *Nicene and Post-Nicene Fathers*, Vol. 4, ed. Philip Schaff and Henry Wace (1892; reprint: Peabody, MA: Hendricksen, 1999), p. 234; emphasis added.

ACKNOWLEDGMENTS

I am surrounded by minds and hands that make my own mind and hands fruitful. I cannot thank God adequately that he has made the lines fall for me in these pleasant places. Being a pastor at Bethlehem Baptist Church is like being planted in rich soil with daily watering and ample sunshine and the addition of ever-fresh nutriment. I bless the day that God called me to the ministry of the Word and set me as an elder in this church.

Justin Taylor has served as an ever-competent, willing editor and research assistant who regularly goes beyond what would be required. I thank God for his partnership over these last six years. Carol Steinbach—with assistance from Greg Sweet, Catherine Tong, and Molly Piper—extends her camaraderie in this cause into a third decade and provides again the useful person and Scripture indexes—and weekly encouragements to me in her role at Desiring God.

My wife Noël has read more Piper books more times than anyone in the world. As I write this, she is sitting in our living room with the manuscript of this book spread out on her lap with a red pen in hand and lots of pink post-its appearing on the edges of the proofs. She has an eagle eye for spelling, dates, grammar, style, and logic. Not much gets by her. Her probing questions don't have the effect of making me feel better. They just make the book better. It is all part of our uncommon union, for which I am deeply thankful to God.

These chapters took their first shape as messages in the Bethlehem Conference for Pastors. There would be no Swan books without that conference. So I feel an indebtedness to the brothers who have come to worship and to learn. These conferences would not happen as they do without the extraordinary gifts and grace of Scott Anderson, the Director for Conferences at Desiring God.

I have dedicated the book to R. C. Sproul, founder of Ligonier Ministries. Dr. Sproul is one of the clearest and most compelling contenders for the fullness of the biblical faith with all its magnificent contours. I rejoice in the centrality and supremacy of God he has so relentlessly and faithfully kept before the church for these last three decades.

Finally, I thank Jesus Christ who loved me and gave himself for me. He is the same yesterday, today, and forever. May we learn from Athanasius, Owen, and Machen to contend well for his cause until he comes.

Men tell us that our preaching should be positive and not negative, that we can preach the truth without attacking error. But if we follow that advice we shall have to close our Bible and desert its teachings. The New Testament is a polemic book almost from beginning to end.

Some years ago I was in a company of teachers of the Bible in the colleges and other educational institutions of America. One of the most eminent theological professors in the country made an address. In it he admitted that there are unfortunate controversies about doctrine in the Epistles of Paul; but, said he in effect, the real essence of Paul's teaching is found in the hymn to Christian love in the thirteenth chapter of I Corinthians; and we can avoid controversy today, if we will only devote the chief attention to that inspiring hymn.

In reply, I am bound to say that the example was singularly ill-chosen. That hymn to Christian love is in the midst of a great polemic passage; it would never have been written if Paul had been opposed to controversy with error in the Church. It was because his soul was stirred within him by a wrong use of the spiritual gifts that he was able to write that glorious hymn. So it is always in the Church. Every really great Christian utterance, it may almost be said, is born in controversy. It is when men have felt compelled to take a stand against error that they have risen to the really great heights in the celebration of truth.

J. GRESHAM MACHEN, "CHRISTIAN SCHOLARSHIP AND THE DEFENSE OF THE FAITH," IN *J. GRESHAM MACHEN: SELECTED SHORTER WRITINGS*, ED. D. G. HART (PHILLIPSBURG, NJ: P&R, 2004), PP. 148-149

INTRODUCTION

Sacred Controversy in Scripture, History, and the Lives of the Swans

Controversy, Cowardice, and Pride

Some controversy is crucial for the sake of life-giving truth. Running from it is a sign of cowardice. But enjoying it is usually a sign of pride. Some necessary tasks are sad, and even victory is not without tears—unless there is pride. The reason enjoying controversy is a sign of pride is that humility loves truth-based unity more than truth-based victory. Humility loves Christ-exalting exultation more than Christ-defending confrontation—even more than Christ-defending vindication. Humility delights to worship Christ in spirit and truth. If it must fight for worship-sustaining truth, it will, but that is not because the fight is pleasant. It's not even because victory is pleasant. It's because knowing and loving and proclaiming Christ for who he really is and what he really did is pleasant.

Indeed knowing and loving the truth of Christ is not only pleasant now, it is the only path to everlasting life and joy. That's why Athanasius (298-373), John Owen (1616-1683), and J. Gresham Machen (1881-1937) took so seriously the controversies of their time. It was not what they liked; but it was what love required—love for Christ and his church and his world.

Controversy Less Crucial, But Necessary

There are more immediately crucial tasks than controversy about the truth and meaning of the gospel. For example, it is more immediately crucial that we believe the gospel, and proclaim it to the unreached, and pray for power to attend the preaching of the gospel. But this is like saying that flying food to starving people is more immediately crucial than the science of aeronautics. True. But the food will not be flown to the needy if someone is not doing aeronautics. It is like saying that giving penicillin shots to children dying of fever is more immediately crucial than the work of biology and chemistry. True. But there would be no penicillin without such work.

In every age there is a kind of person who tries to minimize the importance of truth-defining and truth-defending controversy by saying that prayer, worship, evangelism, missions, and dependence on the Holy Spirit are more important. Who has not heard such rejoinders to controversy: "Let's stop arguing about the gospel and get out there and share it with a dying world." Or: "Prayer is more powerful than argument." Or: "We should rely on the Holy Spirit and not on our reasoning." Or: "God wants to be worshiped, not discussed."

I love the passion for faith and prayer and evangelism and worship behind those statements. But when they are used to belittle gospel-defining, gospel-defending controversy they bite the hand that feeds them. Christ-exalting prayer will not survive in an atmosphere where the preservation and explanation and vindication of the teaching of the Bible about the prayer-hearing God are devalued. Evangelism and world missions must feed on the solid food of well-grounded, unambiguous, rich gospel truth in order to sustain courage and confidence in the face of afflictions and false religions. And corporate worship will be diluted with cultural substitutes where the deep, clear, biblical contours of God's glory are not seen and guarded from ever-encroaching error.

It is not valid to contrast dependence on the Holy Spirit with the defense of his Word in controversy. The reason is that the Holy Spirit uses means—including the preaching and defending of the gospel. J. Gresham Machen put it like this:

> It is perfectly true, of course, that argument alone is quite insufficient to make a man a Christian. You may argue with him from now until the end of the world; you may bring forth the most magnificent arguments—but all will be in vain unless there is one other thing: the mysterious, creative power of the Holy Spirit in the new birth. But because argument is insufficient, it does not follow that it is unnecessary. Sometimes it is used directly by the Holy Spirit to bring a man to Christ. But more frequently it is used indirectly.[1]

This is why Athanasius, John Owen, and J. Gresham Machen engaged their minds and hearts and lives in the Christ-defining and Christ-defending controversies of their day. It was not because the Holy Spirit and prayer were inadequate. It was because the Holy Spirit works through the Word preached and explained and defended. It was because biblical prayer aims not just at the heart of the person who needs persuading, but also at the per-

---

[1] J. Gresham Machen, "Christian Scholarship and the Defense of the Faith," in *J. Gresham Machen: Selected Shorter Writings*, ed. D. G. Hart (Phillipsburg, NJ: P&R, 2004), pp. 144-145. One should also recall how Paul "reasoned" in the synagogues in order to win converts by the power of the Holy Spirit (Acts 17:2, 17; 18:4, 19; 24:25).

suader.[2] The Holy Spirit makes a biblical argument compelling in the mouth of the teacher and in the heart of the student.

And Athanasius, Owen, and Machen believed that what they were contending for was of infinite worth. It was indeed not a distraction from the work of love. It was love—love to Christ, his church, and his world.

Controversy When "Our All" Is at Stake

In Athanasius's lifelong battle for the deity of Christ against the Arians, who said that Christ was created, Athanasius said, "Considering that *this struggle is for our all* . . . let us also make it our earnest care and aim to guard what we have received."[3] When *all* is at stake, it is worth contending. This is what love does.

Machen, in his twentieth-century American situation, put it like this: "Controversy of the right sort is good; for out of such controversy, as Church history and Scripture alike teach, there comes the salvation of souls."[4] When you believe that *soul-saving* truth (our *all*) is at stake in a controversy, running away is not only cowardly but cruel. These men never ran.

John Owen, the greatest Puritan intellect, took up more controversies than Machen and Athanasius combined, but was driven by an even more manifest love for Christ. Not that he loved Christ more (only God can know that); but he articulated the battle for

---

[2] Second Thessalonians 3:1, "Finally, brothers, pray for us, that the word of the Lord may speed ahead and be honored." Colossians 4:3, "Pray also for us, that God may open to us a door for the word." Ephesians 6:19, "[Pray] for me, that words may be given to me in opening my mouth boldly to proclaim the mystery of the gospel."

[3] *Athanasius: Select Works and Letters*, in *Nicene and Post-Nicene Fathers* (NPNF), ed. Philip Schaff and Henry Wace (1892; reprint: Peabody, MA: Hendricksen, 1999), 4:234. Emphasis added.

[4] J. Gresham Machen, *What Is Faith?* (1925; reprint: Edinburgh: Banner of Truth, 1991), pp. 42-43.

communion with Christ more explicitly than they. For Owen, virtually every confrontation with error was for the sake of the contemplation of Christ. Communion with Christ was his constant theme and goal. He held the view that such contemplation and communion were only possible by means of true views of Christ. Truth about Christ was necessary for communion with Christ.

Therefore all controversy in the defense of this truth was for the sake of worship.

> What soul that hath any acquaintance with these things falls not down with reverence and astonishment? How glorious is he that is the Beloved of our souls! . . . When . . . our life, our peace, our joy, our inheritance, our eternity, *our all,* lies herein, shall not the thoughts of it always dwell in our hearts, always refresh and delight our souls?[5]

As with Athanasius, Owen said that "our all" is at stake in contending for the truth of Christ. Then he brings the battle into the closest connection with the blessing of communion with God. Even *in* the battle, not just *after* it, we must commune with God. "When we have *communion with God in the doctrine we contend for*—then shall we be garrisoned by the grace of God against all the assaults of men."[6] The aim of contending for Christ is also essential to the means. If we do not delight in Christ through the truth that we defend, our defense is not for the sake of the preciousness of Christ. The end and the means of Christ-exalting controversy is worship.

---

[5] John Owen, *Of Communion with God,* in *The Works of John Owen,* 24 vols., ed. William Goold (1850-1853; reprint: Edinburgh: Banner of Truth, 1965), 2:69. Emphasis added.
[6] Owen, *Works,* 1:lxiii-lxiv. Emphasis added.

A Mistaken Notion About Controversy and Church Vitality

There is a mistaken notion about the relationship between the health of the church and the presence of controversy. For example, some say that spiritual awakening and power and growth will not come to the church of Christ until church leaders lay aside doctrinal differences and come together in prayer. Indeed there should be much corporate prayer for God's mercy on us. And indeed there are some doctrinal differences that should not be elevated to a place of prominence. Machen explained his own passion for doctrine with this caution: "We do not mean, in insisting upon the doctrinal basis of Christianity, that all points of doctrine are equally important. It is perfectly possible for Christian fellowship to be maintained despite differences of opinion."[7]

But there is a historical and biblical error in the assumption that the church will not grow and prosper in times of controversy. Machen said, as we saw above, that church history and Scripture teach the value of right controversy. This is important to see, because if we do not see it, we will yield to the massive pragmatic pressure of our time to minimize doctrine. We will cave in to the pressure that a truth-driven ministry cannot be a people-loving, soul-saving, church-reviving, justice-advancing, missions-mobilizing, worship-intensifying, Christ-exalting ministry. But, in fact, it is truth—biblical truth, doctrinal truth—that gives foundation and duration to all these things.

---

[7] J. Gresham Machen, *Christianity and Liberalism* (1923; reprint: Grand Rapids, MI: Eerdmans, 1992), p. 48.

The Witness of Church History to the Place of Controversy

The witness of church history is that seasons of controversy have often been seasons of growth and strength. This was the case in the first centuries of the church. Most Christians today would be stunned if they knew that the battle for the deity of Christ was not a battle between the great force of orthodoxy, on the one hand, and marginal heretics, on the other. It was a battle in which at times the majority of the church leaders in the world were unorthodox.[8] Yet the church grew in spite of controversy and persecution. Indeed I believe we must say that the growth of the true church in those days was *because of* leaders like Athanasius, who took a stand for the sake of truth. Without controversy there would have been no gospel, and therefore no church.

The Protestant Reformation

The time of the Protestant Reformation was a time of great controversy both between the Protestants and Roman Catholics and between the Reformers themselves. Yet the fullness of the gospel was preserved in these great doctrinal battles, and true faith spread and was strengthened. In fact, the spread and vitality of the Reformed faith in the century after John Calvin's death in 1564 was astonishing[9] and produced some of the greatest pastors and

---

[8] The Council of Nicaea did not settle the issue of Christ's deity—it drew the battle lines. The majority of bishops who signed it (all but two) were politically motivated. "In the years immediately following, we find a large majority of the Eastern bishops, especially of Syria and Asia Minor, the very regions whence the numerical strength of the council was drawn, in full reaction against the council." *NPNF,* 4:xxi.

[9] German Calvinist Abraham Scultetus (1566-1624) described the spread of Reformed influence thirty years after Calvin's death. "I cannot fail to recall the optimistic mood which I and many others felt when we considered the condition of the Reformed churches in 1591. In France there ruled the valiant King Henri IV, in England the mighty Queen Elizabeth, in Scotland the learned King James, in the Palatinate the bold hero John Casimir, in Saxony the courageous and powerful Elector Christian I, in Hesse the clever and prudent Landgrave William, who were

theologians the world has ever known[10]—all of this born in the controversies of Wittenberg and Geneva.

The First Great Awakening

The First Great Awakening in Britain and America in the eighteenth century was a time of tremendous growth for the church and of profound awakening of thousands of individuals. But it is common knowledge that the two greatest itinerant preachers in this movement were opposed to each other's understanding of God's work in salvation. George Whitefield was a Calvinist, and John Wesley was an Arminian.

J. I. Packer explains the five points of Calvinism in this way:

> (1) Fallen man in his natural state lacks all power to believe the gospel, just as he lacks all power to believe the law, despite all external inducements that may be extended to him. (2) God's election is a free, sovereign, unconditional choice of sinners, as sinners, to be redeemed by Christ, given faith, and brought to glory. (3) The redeeming work of Christ had as its end and goal the salvation of the elect. (4) The work of the Holy Spirit in bringing men to faith never fails to achieve its object. (5) Believers are kept in faith and grace by the unconquerable power of God till they come to glory. These five points are conveniently

---

all inclined to Reformed religion. In the Netherlands everything went as Prince Maurice of Orange wished, when he took Breda, Zutphen, Hulst, and Nijmegen. . . . We imagined that *aureum seculum*, a golden age, had dawned." Quoted in Alister E. McGrath, *A Life of John Calvin* (Grand Rapids, MI: Baker, 1990), p. 199.

[10] When I speak of notable pastors and theologians, I am thinking mainly of the pastoral theologians called Puritans who flourished in Great Britain in the century following John Calvin's death. J. I. Packer called these pastor-theologians the "Redwoods" of church history. "California's Redwoods make me think of England's Puritans, another breed of giants who in our time have begun to be newly appreciated. Between 1550 and 1700 they too lived unfrilled lives in which, speaking spiritually, strong growth and resistance to fire and storm were what counted." *A Quest For Godliness: The Puritan Vision of the Christian Life* (Wheaton, IL: Crossway Books, 1990), p. 11.

denoted by the mnemonic TULIP: Total depravity, Unconditional election, Limited atonement, Irresistible grace, Preservation of the saints.

And here is how Packer unpacks the five points of Arminianism:

(1) Man is never so completely corrupted by sin that he cannot savingly believe the gospel when it is put before him, nor (2) is he ever so completely controlled by God that he cannot reject it. (3) God's election of those who shall be saved is prompted by his foreseeing that they will of their own accord believe. (4) Christ's death did not ensure the salvation of anyone, for it did not secure the gift of faith to anyone (there is no such gift): what it did was rather to create a possibility of salvation for everyone if they believe. (5) It rests with believers to keep themselves in a state of grace by keeping up their faith; those who fail here fall away and are lost. Thus, Arminianism made man's salvation depend ultimately on man himself, saving faith being viewed throughout as man's own work and, because his own, not God's in him.[11]

At the human center of the Great Awakening was controversy. Wesley's disagreement with Calvinism "burst forth in a sermon from 1740 titled 'Free Grace.' . . . For Wesley the Calvinist insistence that God's electing power was the basic element in the sinner's conversion verged dangerously close to antinomianism. . . . Wesley could not be persuaded that the Bible taught Calvinist doctrines."[12]

---

[11] Ibid., p. 128.
[12] Mark A. Noll, *The Rise of Evangelicalism: The Age of Edwards, Whitefield, and the Wesleys* (Downers Grove, IL: InterVarsity Press, 2003), p. 122.

Whitefield responded to Wesley's criticism with a published letter from Bethesda, Georgia, dated December 24, 1740. He knew that controversy between evangelicals would be frowned upon by some and savored by others. Yet he felt compelled to engage in the controversy:

> I am very apprehensive that our common adversaries will rejoice to see us differing among ourselves. But what can I say? The children of God are in danger of falling into error. . . . When I remember how Paul reproved Peter for his dissimulation, I fear I have been sinfully silent too long. Oh! then, be not angry with me, dear and honored sir, if now I deliver my soul, by telling you that I think, in this you greatly err.[13]

Mark Noll said that Whitefield's response to Wesley "inaugurated the most enduring theological conflict among evangelicals, the conflict between Arminian and Calvinist interpretations of Scripture on the nature, motive powers and implications of salvation."[14] Nevertheless, with controversy at the center, the Great Awakening brought unprecedented life and growth to churches in the American colonies and Britain. Take the Baptists, for example. They were the "primary beneficiaries of the Great Awakening"[15] in America. "In the colonies of North America there were less than one hundred Baptist churches in 1740, but almost five hundred by the outbreak of the war with Britain in 1776."[16] Similarly the Presbyterian churches rose from about

---

[13] George Whitefield, "A Letter From George Whitefield to the Rev. Mr. John Wesley, in Answer to Mr. Wesley's Sermon Entitled 'Free Grace,'" (December 24, 1740), in *George Whitefield's Journals* (Edinburgh: Banner of Truth, 1960), p. 569ff.

[14] Noll, *The Rise of Evangelicalism*, p. 122.

[15] Ibid., p. 183.

[16] Ibid.

160 in 1740 to nearly six hundred by 1776.[17] The point is that controversy was prominent in the Great Awakening, and God blessed the movement with spiritual life and growth.

The Second Great Awakening

The same thing can be said of the Second Great Awakening. It was "the most influential revival of Christianity in the history of the United States. Its very size and its many expressions have led some historians to question whether a *single* Second Great Awakening can be identified as such. Yet from about 1795 to about 1810 there was a broad and general rekindling of interest in Christianity through the country."[18] Francis Asbury and Charles Finney were the main leaders of this Awakening. Both were controversial, and both saw amazing growth.

When Francis Asbury came to America in 1771, four Methodist ministers were caring for about three hundred laypeople. When he died in 1816, there were two thousand ministers and over two hundred thousand Methodists in the States and several thousand more in Canada.[19] But his attachment to the Englishman John Wesley and his unorthodox methods of ministry brought Asbury into controversy with American patriots and church leaders. For example, he was banished from Maryland because he would not sign an oath of loyalty to the new state government.[20] The blessing of God on his ministry for forty-five years was unbroken by the controversy that swirled around it.

---

[17] Ibid., p. 185.
[18] Mark A. Noll, *A History of Christianity in the United States and Canada* (Grand Rapids, MI: Eerdmans, 1992), p. 166.
[19] Ibid, p. 173.
[20] Ibid., p. 171.

Finney, who broke with his Presbyterian background, was unorthodox both in method and theology. He took over the use of the controversial "anxious bench" and made it into a norm of later revivalism.[21] He was more Arminian than John Wesley:

> Wesley maintained that the human will is incapable of choosing God apart from God's preparatory grace, but Finney rejected this requirement. He was a perfectionist who believed that a permanent stage of higher spiritual life was possible for anyone who sought it wholeheartedly. Following the theologians of New England, he held a governmental view of the atonement whereby Christ's death was a public demonstration of God's willingness to forgive sins rather than payment for sin itself.[22]

This kind of theology was bound to meet opposition. One example of that controversy can be seen by observing Finney's relationship with his contemporaries Asahel Nettleton and Lyman Beecher. "Finney was the spokesman for the surging frontier religion which was both speculative and emotional. Nettleton was the defender of the old New England orthodoxy which refused to be shaken from the moorings of the past."[23] Lyman Beecher was a Congregational pastor in Boston and shared Nettleton's historic Calvinist views. Both these men had fruitful ministries, and Nettleton's itinerant evangelism was blessed with so many con-

---

[21] Ibid., p. 176.
[22] Ibid., p. 177. Finney also rejected the doctrine of original sin and the imputation of Christ's righteousness. "I insisted that our reason was given for the very purpose of enabling us to justify the ways of God; and that no such fiction of imputation could by any possibility be true." Quoted in J. F. Thornbury, *God Sent Revival: The Story of Asahel Nettleton and the Second Great Awakening* (Grand Rapids, MI: Evangelical Press, 1977), p. 160.
[23] Thornbury, *God Sent Revival*, p. 168.

versions that Francis Wayland (1796-1865), an early president of Brown University, said, "I suppose no minister of his time was the means of so many conversions. . . . He . . . would sway an audience as the trees of the forest are moved by a mighty wind."[24]

But the controversy between Finney, on the one hand, and Nettleton and Beecher, on the other, was so intense that a meeting was called in New Lebanon, New York, in 1827 to work out the differences. Numerous concerned clergy came from both the Finney and the Beecher side. It ended without reconciliation, and Beecher said to Finney, "Finney, I know your plan, and you know I do; you mean to come to Connecticut and carry a streak of fire to Boston. But if you attempt it, as the Lord liveth, I'll meet you at the State line, and call out all the artillery men, and fight every inch of the way to Boston, and then I'll fight you there."[25]

Controversy and Vitality and Growth Are Compatible

The point of these illustrations from church history is to lay to rest the notion that powerful spiritual awakening can only come when controversy is put aside. Though I would not want to press it as a strategy, history seems to suggest the opposite. When there is a great movement of God to bring revival and reformation to his church, controversy becomes part of the human process. It would

---

[24] Ibid., p. 55. The reason Wayland could say this, in spite of Finney's amazing success, was that Nettleton's converts had a remarkable reputation of remaining faithful over time and proving themselves true converts, while Finney's were more like the converts of mass evangelism in our own day—a large percentage fell away. "Given the extent of his exposure, and the permanence of his converts, he may well have been, next to George Whitefield, the most effective evangelist in the history of the United States. The ratio of his converts to the population of America in his day [about nine million] is very revealing. Although there is no way of knowing how many were brought to salvation through his preaching, a conservative estimate would be twenty-five thousand. Based on the reports of firsthand witnesses, and pastors who labored in the communities where his revivals took place, sometimes examining the situation thirty years later, only a small fraction of these converts were spurious." Ibid., p. 233.
[25] Ibid., p. 178.

not be far off to say with Parker Williamson that at least in some
instances the controversy was not just a result but a means of the
revitalization of the church.

> Historically, controversies that have swirled around
> the meaning and implications of the Gospel, far from
> damaging the Church, have contributed to its vitality.
> Like a refiner's fire, intense theological debate has
> resulted in clarified belief, common vision, and invigo-
> rated ministry.[26]

J. Gresham Machen came to the same conclusion as he looked
over the history of the church and the nature of Christ's mission in
the world:

> Every true revival is born in controversy, and leads to more
> controversy. That has been true ever since our Lord said
> that he came not to bring peace upon the earth but a
> sword. And do you know what I think will happen when
> God sends a new reformation upon the church? We cannot
> tell when that blessed day will come. But when the blessed
> day does come, I think we can say at least one result that
> it will bring. We shall hear nothing on that day about the
> evils of controversy in the church. All that will be swept
> away as with a mighty flood. A man who is on fire with a
> message never talks in that wretched, feeble way, but pro-
> claims the truth joyously and fearlessly, in the presence of
> every high thing that is lifted up against the gospel of
> Christ.[27]

---

[26] Parker T. Williamson, *Standing Firm: Reclaiming Christian Faith in Times of Controversy*
(Springfield, PA: PLC Publications, 1996), p. 2.
[27] Ned B. Stonehouse, *J. Gresham Machen: A Biographical Memoir* (1954, reprint: Edinburgh:
Banner of Truth Trust, 1987), p. 148.

Probably the regular presence of controversy in times of revival and reformation is owing to several factors. In these seasons of emerging spiritual life, passions run higher. And when passions are higher, controversy is more likely. Satan too can see the dangers of revival to his cause and will surely work to bring disunity and disrepute on the leaders if he can. But more essentially, awakening and reformation are caused and carried by more clear perception of the glories of Christ and the repugnance of sin; and when these are seen more clearly and spoken of more precisely, division is more likely than when Christ is spoken of in vague terms and people care little for his name. Add to this that in times of revival people see more clearly that eternity is at stake in what we believe, and this gives a cutting edge to doctrine. It really matters when you see that "our all" is at stake.

The Witness of Scripture to the Place of Controversy

In addition to church history, the Bible itself testifies that there is a body of doctrine about God and his ways that exists objectively outside ourselves, and that this truth is so important that preserving it is worth controversy if necessary. The apostle Paul calls this body of doctrine "the standard of teaching to which you were committed" (Romans 6:17). That's the way it functions. It is a standard, a yardstick, a pattern. You measure all other truth by it. Elsewhere he calls it "the whole counsel of God" (Acts 20:27) and the "pattern of the sound words" and "the good deposit entrusted to you" (2 Timothy 1:13-14). In other words, it doesn't change.

The importance of this revealed truth about God and his ways can hardly be overemphasized. It awakens and sustains faith;[28] it is the source of obedience;[29] it frees from sin;[30] it liberates from Satan's bondage;[31] it awakens and sustains love;[32] it saves;[33] it sustains joy.[34] And most of all—as the sum of all the rest—this body of biblical truth is the means of having God the Father and God the Son: "Whoever abides in the teaching has both the Father and the Son" (2 John 9).

The reason Christianity has been so uncongenial to the pragmatic mind-set that resists controversy at all costs is that at the core of Christian faith are history and doctrine that do not change. Machen states with characteristic clarity:

> From the beginning, the Christian gospel, as indeed the name "gospel" or "good news" implies, consisted in an account of something that had happened. And from the beginning, the meaning of the happening was set forth; and when the meaning of the happening was set forth then there was Christian doctrine. "Christ died"—that is

---

[28] Romans 10:17, "So faith comes from hearing, and hearing through the word of Christ."

[29] John 17:17, "Sanctify them in the truth; Your word is truth." Second Peter 1:3-4, "His divine power has granted to us everything pertaining to life and godliness, through the true knowledge of Him who called us by His own glory and excellence. For by these He has granted to us His precious and magnificent promises, so that by them you may become partakers of *the* divine nature, having escaped the corruption that is in the world by lust" (NASB).

[30] John 8:32, "and you will know the truth, and the truth will set you free."

[31] Second Timothy 2:24-26, "The Lord's bond-servant must not be quarrelsome, but be kind to all, able to teach, patient when wronged, with gentleness correcting those who are in opposition, if perhaps God may grant them repentance leading to the knowledge of the truth, and they may come to their senses *and escape* from the snare of the devil, having been held captive by him to do his will" (NASB).

[32] Philippians 1:9, "And this I pray, that your love may abound still more and more in real knowledge and all discernment" (NASB).

[33] First Timothy 4:16, "Pay close attention to yourself and to your teaching; persevere in these things, for as you do this you will ensure salvation both for yourself and for those who hear you" (NASB). Acts 20:26-27, "I testify to you this day that I am innocent of the blood of all men. For I did not shrink from declaring to you the whole purpose of God" (NASB). Second Thessalonians 2:9-10, "The coming of the lawless one is . . . and with all the deception of wickedness for those who perish, because they did not receive the love of the truth so as to be saved."

[34] John 15:11, "These things I have spoken to you, that my joy may be in you, and that your joy may be full."

history; "Christ died for our sins"—that is doctrine. Without these two elements joined in an absolutely indissoluble union, there is no Christianity.[35]

This is why controversy comes. Attempts to "reinterpret" the biblical happening or the biblical interpretation of the happening—the history or the doctrine—are a threat to the heart of Christianity. Christianity is not merely a life or a morality. It is God acting once for all in history, and God interpreting the meaning of those actions in Scripture.

The magnitude of what is at stake in preserving the true meaning of Scripture is so great that controversy is a price faithful teachers have been willing to pay from the very beginning. It is fair to say that we would not have the New Testament if there had been no controversy in the early church. If you remove the documents from the New Testament that were not addressing controversy you will, at most, have a tiny handful from the twenty-seven books.[36]

---

[35] Machen, *Christianity and Liberalism*, p. 27.

[36] Here is a sampling of the controversies we find in the New Testament: Jesus' controversy over paying taxes to Caesar (Mark 12:14-17), whether there is marriage in the resurrection (Matthew 22:23-32), what the greatest commandment is (Matthew 22:36-40), when divorce is permitted (Matthew 5:31-32; 19:9), who the Son of Man is (Matthew 16:13). The controversy in Acts over the feeding of the Hellenistic widows (6:1-6) and over whether circumcision is required for salvation (15). The controversies of Paul over whether we should do evil, that good may come (Romans 3:8), and why God still finds fault when he is the ruler of human wills (Romans 9:19), and whether all days should be esteemed alike (Romans 14:5), and how to handle immorality in the church (1 Corinthians 5), and whether to go to court before unbelieving judges (1 Corinthians 6), and whether singleness is better than marriage, or whether a believer should marry an unbeliever (1 Corinthians 7), and whether meat offered to idols should be eaten by believers (1 Corinthians 8), and whether women may pray and prophesy in public services (1 Corinthians 14:34-35), and how the gift of tongues and prophecy should be used (1 Corinthians 12—14), and whether the dead are raised bodily from the dead (1 Corinthians 15), and whether one should add works to faith as an instrument of justification (Galatians 3—5), and with those professing Christians who want to make his imprisonment harder and worship their bellies (Philippians 1, 3), and with those who accused him of flattery (1 Thessalonians 2:5), and with those who said that the day of the Lord had already come (2 Thessalonians 2), and with those who demanded that food and marriage be avoided (1 Timothy 4:3), and with those who say godliness is a means of gain (1 Timothy 6:5). And then there are all the controversies referred to in the letters of John and Peter and the book of Revelation. But this is enough to show how the earliest church was riddled with controversy.

The New Testament Summons to Controversy

Not only is the New Testament an *example* of controversy, it is also a *summons* to controversy, when controversy is necessary. Jude, the brother of the Lord, says, "I found it necessary to write appealing to you *to contend* for the faith that was once for all delivered to the saints" (Jude 3).

The apostle Paul rejoices that the Philippians are his partners in "the *defense* and confirmation of the gospel" (Philippians 1:7). He charges Timothy to "preach the word. . . . For the time is coming when people will not endure sound teaching, but having itching ears they will accumulate for themselves teachers to suit their own passions, and will turn away from listening to the truth and wander off into myths" (2 Timothy 4:2-4).

Notice that these are church members, not people in the world, who will depart from sound teaching. "*From among your own selves,*" Paul warns the elders of Ephesus, "will arise men speaking twisted things, to draw away the disciples after them" (Acts 20:30). And, as the apostle Peter says, "There will be false teachers *among you,* who will secretly bring in destructive heresies" (2 Peter 2:1). Therefore, Paul concludes soberly, "There must be factions among you in order that those who are genuine among you may be recognized" (1 Corinthians 11:19).

So Let Us Learn from Those Who Have Contended Well

In view of the witness of church history and Scripture to the necessity of controversy in this imperfect world, and the compatibility of controversy and revitalization, we will do well to learn as much as we can from those who have walked through controversy and blessed the church in doing so. Athanasius and Owen and Machen have done that. The lessons they have to teach us are many. Their lives instruct us in the subtleties of how language is manipulated in controversy, and how personal holiness and communion with God is essential in the battle, and how love and patience with our adversaries can sometimes conquer better than argument, and how perseverance through suffering is essential to long-term faithfulness to truth, and how larger cultural issues shape church disputes, and how important it is to out-rejoice the adversary if we claim to contend for good news.

I hope that you will come to love these three brothers who have gone before. I pray that you will count them among the number referred to in Hebrews 13:7, "Remember your leaders, those who spoke to you the word of God. Consider the outcome of their way of life, and imitate their faith." They are worthy in their own right to be emulated—not without reservation—they are mere men. But time has tested them and their work. And it is worth our attention. It is a bonus—a very large one—that all three are from outside our own century (the fourth, seventeenth, and early twentieth). In this way we see reality through the eyes of a different time. That is a great advantage. It serves to liberate us from the dangers of chronological snobbery that assumes ours is the wisest of times.

And as we learn from the heroes of our faith, let us resolve to renounce all controversy-loving pride and all controversy-fearing cowardice. And with humility and courage (that is, with faith in the sovereign Christ) let us heed Martin Luther's warning not to proclaim only what is safe while the battle rages around what is necessary:

If I profess with the loudest voice and clearest exposition every portion of the truth of God except precisely that little point which the world and the devil are at that moment attacking, I am not confessing Christ, however boldly I may be professing Christ. Where the battle rages there the loyalty of the soldier is proved, and to be steady on all the battlefield besides is mere flight and disgrace if he flinches at that point.[37]

---

[37] Quoted in Parker T. Williamson, *Standing Firm: Reclaiming Christian Faith in Times of Controversy* (Springfield, PA: PLC Publications, 1996), p. 5.

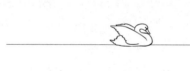

And, in a word, the achievements of the Savior, resulting from His becoming man, are of such kind and number, that if one should wish to enumerate them, he may be compared to men who gaze at the expanse of the sea and wish to count its waves.

For as one cannot take in the whole of the waves with his eyes, for those which are coming on baffle the sense of him that attempts it; so for him that would take in all the achievements of Christ in the body, it is impossible to take in the whole, even by reckoning them up, as those which go beyond his thought are more than those he thinks he has taken in.

Better is it, then, not to aim at speaking of the whole, where one cannot do justice even to a part, but, after mentioning one more, to leave the whole for you to marvel at. For all alike are marvelous, and wherever a man turns his glance, he may behold on that side the divinity of the Word, and be struck with exceeding great awe.

ATHANASIUS, ON THE INCARNATION OF THE WORD, NICENE AND POST-NICENE FATHERS, VOL. 4, (PEABODY, MA: HENDRICKSEN, 1999), PP. 65-66

1

CONTENDING FOR CHRIST
CONTRA MUNDUM

Exile and Incarnation in the Life of Athanasius

Best-Loved Bishop

Athanasius was born in A.D. 298 in Egypt and became the bishop of Alexandria on June 8, 328 at the age of thirty. The people of Egypt viewed him as their bishop until he died on May 2, 373, at the age of seventy-five.[1] I say he was "viewed" by the people as their bishop during these years because Athanasius was driven out of his church and office five times by the powers of the Roman Empire. Seventeen of his forty-five years as bishop were spent in exile. But the people never acknowledged the validity of the other bishops sent to take his place. He was always bishop in exile as far as his flock was concerned.

Gregory of Nazianzus (330-389) gave a memorial sermon in Constantinople seven years after the death of Athanasius and described the affections of the Egyptian people for their bishop.

---

[1] Timothy D. Barnes, *Athanasius and Constantius: Theology and Politics in the Constantinian Empire* (Cambridge, MA: Harvard University Press, 1993), p. 19.

Gregory tells us that when Athanasius returned from his third exile in 364, having been gone for six years, he arrived

> amid such delight of the people of the city and of almost all Egypt, that they ran together from every side, from the furthest limits of the country, simply to hear the voice of Athanasius, or feast their eyes upon the sight of him.[2]

From their standpoint none of the foreign appointments to the office of bishop in Alexandria for forty-five years was valid but one, Athanasius. This devotion was owing to the kind of man Athanasius was. Gregory remembered him like this:

> Let one praise him in his fastings and prayers . . . another his unweariedness and zeal for vigils and psalmody, another his patronage of the needy, another his dauntlessness towards the powerful, or his condescension to the lowly. . . . [He was to] the unfortunate their consolation, the hoary-headed their staff, youths their instructor, the poor their resource, the wealthy their steward. Even the widows will . . . praise their protector, even the orphans their father, even the poor their benefactor, strangers their entertainer, brethren the man of brotherly love, the sick their physician.[3]

One of the things that makes that kind of praise from a contemporary the more credible is that, unlike many ancient saints, Athanasius is not recorded as having done any miracles. Archibald Robertson, who edited Athanasius's works for *Nicene and Post-*

---

[2] Gregory of Nazianzus, *Oration 21: On Athanasius of Alexandria*, in Gregory Nazianzus, *Select Orations, Sermons, Letters; Dogmatic Treatises*, in *Nicene and Post-Nicene Fathers* [*NPNF*], Vol. 7, 2nd Series, ed. Philip Shaff and Henry Wace (reprint: Grand Rapids, MI: Eerdmans, 1955), p. 277 ¶27.

[3] Ibid., p. 272 ¶10.

Nicene Fathers, said, "He is . . . surrounded by an atmosphere of truth. Not a single miracle of any kind is related of him. . . . The saintly reputation of Athanasius rested on his life and character alone, without the aid of any reputation for miraculous power."[4] Then he goes on with his own praise of Athanasius:

> In the whole of our minute knowledge of his life there is a total lack of self-interest. The glory of God and the welfare of the Church absorbed him fully at all times. . . . The Emperors recognized him as a political force of the first order . . . but on no occasion does he yield to the temptation of using the arm of flesh. Almost unconscious of his own power . . . his humility is the more real for never being conspicuously paraded. . . . Courage, self-sacrifice, steadiness of purpose, versatility and resourcefulness, width of ready sympathy, were all harmonized by deep reverence and the discipline of a single-minded lover of Christ.[5]

Athanasius: Father of Orthodoxy Contra Mundum

This single-minded love for Jesus Christ expressed itself in a life-long battle to explain and defend Christ's deity and to worship Christ as Lord and God. This is what Athanasius is best known for. There were times when it seemed the whole world had abandoned orthodoxy. That is why the phrase *Athanasius contra mundum* (against the world) arose. He stood steadfast against overwhelming defection from orthodoxy, and only at the end of his life could he see the dawn of triumph.

But in a sense it is anachronistic to use the word *orthodoxy*

---

[4] *NPNF*, 4:lxvii.
[5] Ibid.

this way—to say that the world *abandoned* orthodoxy. Was it already there to abandon? Of course, biblical truth is always there to abandon. But *orthodoxy* generally refers to a historic or official or universally held view of what is true to Scripture. Was *that* there to abandon? The answer is suggested in the other great name given to Athanasius, namely, "Father of Orthodoxy."[6] That phrase seems to say that orthodoxy came to be because of Athanasius. And in one sense that is true in regard to the doctrine of the Trinity. The relationships between the Father and the Son and the Holy Spirit had not received formal statement in any representative council before the time of Athanasius.

R. P. C. Hanson wrote, "There was not as yet any orthodox doctrine [of the Trinity], for if there had been, the controversy could hardly have lasted sixty years before resolution."[7] The sixty years he has in mind is the time between the Council of Nicaea in 325 and the Council of Constantinople[8] in 381. The Council of Nicaea established the battle lines and staked out the deity of Christ, and the Council of Constantinople confirmed and refined the Nicene Creed. In the intervening sixty years there was doctrinal war over whether the Nicene formulation would stand and become "orthodoxy."

This was the war Athanasius fought for forty-five years. It lasted all his life, but the orthodox outcome was just over the horizon when he died in 373. And under God this outcome was owing to the courage and constancy and work and writing of

---

[6] Ibid., p. lviii.
[7] R. P. C. Hanson, *The Search for the Christian Doctrine of God: The Arian Controversy* (Edinburgh: T. & T. Clark, 1988), pp. xviii-xix.
[8] See the chapter on "The Council of Constantinople" in Robert Letham, *The Holy Trinity: In Scripture, History, Theology, and Worship* (Phillipsburg, NJ: P&R, 2004), pp. 167-183.

Athanasius. No one comes close to his influence in the cause of biblical truth during his lifetime.[9]

Arius Fires the Shot Heard 'Round the Roman World

The war was sparked in A.D. 319. A deacon in Alexandria named Arius, who had been born in 256 in Libya, presented a letter to Bishop Alexander arguing that if the Son of God were truly a Son, he must have had a beginning. There must have been a time, therefore, when he did not exist. Most of what we know of Arius is from others. All we have from Arius's own pen are three letters, a fragment of a fourth, and a scrap of a song, the *Thalia*.[10] In fact he proved to be a very minor character in the controversy he unleashed. He died in 336.[11]

Athanasius was a little over twenty when the controversy broke out—over forty years younger than Arius (a lesson in how the younger generation may be more biblically faithful than the older[12]). Athanasius was in the service of Alexander, the bishop

---

[9] "The Nicene formula found in Athanasius a mind predisposed to enter into its spirit, to employ in its defense the richest resources of theological and biblical training, of spiritual depth and vigor, of self-sacrificing but sober and tactful enthusiasm; *its victory in the East is due under God to him alone.*" *NPNF*, 4:lxix.

[10] Letham, *The Holy Trinity*, p. 109.

[11] Archibald Robertson recounts the death of Arius like this: "From Jerusalem Arius had gone to Alexandria, but had not succeeded in obtaining admission to the Communion of the Church there. Accordingly he repaired to the capital about the time of the Council [of Tyre]. The Eusebians resolved that here at any rate he should not be repelled. Arius appeared before the Emperor and satisfied him by a sworn profession of orthodoxy, and a day was fixed for his reception to communion. The story of the distress caused to the aged bishop Alexander [Bishop of Constantinople] is well known. He was heard to pray in the church that either Arius or himself might be taken away before such an outrage to the faith should be permitted. As a matter of fact Arius died suddenly [A.D. 336] the day before his intended reception. His friends ascribed his death to magic, those of Alexander to the judgment of God, the public generally to the effect of excitement on a diseased heart. Athanasius, while taking the second view, describes the occurrence with becoming sobriety and reserve (pp. 233, 565)." *NPNF* 4:xli.

[12] The Bible encourages us to hold older people in honor. "You shall stand up before the gray head and honor the face of an old man, and you shall fear your God: I am the LORD" (Leviticus 19:32). In general, wisdom is found with age and experience (1 Kings 12:8), but not always. Timothy is exhorted in 1 Timothy 4:12, "Let no one despise you for your youth." There are situations when he would have to correct the elderly (1 Timothy 5:1). And in the book of Job

of Alexandria. Almost nothing is known of his youth. Gregory of Nazianzus celebrates the fact that Athanasius was brought up mainly in biblical rather than philosophical training.

> He was brought up, from the first, in religious habits and practices, after a brief study of literature and philosophy, so that he might not be utterly unskilled in such subjects, or ignorant of matters which he had determined to despise. For his generous and eager soul could not brook being occupied in vanities, like unskilled athletes, who beat the air instead of their antagonists and lose the prize. From meditating on every book of the Old and New Testament, with a depth such as none else has applied even to one of them, he grew rich in contemplation, rich in splendor of life.[13]

This was the service he was to render for forty-five years: biblical blow after blow against the fortresses of the Arian heresy. Robert Letham confirms the outcome of Gregory's observation: "Athanasius' contribution to the theology of the Trinity can scarcely be overestimated. . . . He turned discussion away from philosophical speculation and back to a biblical and theological basis."[14]

In 321 a synod was convened in Alexandria, and Arius was deposed from his office and his views declared heresy. Athanasius at age twenty-three wrote the deposition for Alexander. This was to be his role now for the next fifty-two years—writing to declare the glories of the incarnate Son of God. The deposition of Arius

---

the young Elihu proved to be wiser than Job's three older friends. "Now Elihu had waited to speak to Job because they were older than he. And when Elihu saw that there was no answer in the mouth of these three men, he burned with anger. And Elihu the son of Barachel the Buzite answered and said: 'I am young in years, and you are aged; therefore I was timid and afraid to declare my opinion to you. I said, "Let days speak, and many years teach wisdom." But it is the spirit in man, the breath of the Almighty, that makes him understand. It is not the old who are wise, nor the aged who understand what is right'" (Job 32:4-9).

[13] Gregory of Nazianzus, *Oration 21*, pp. 270-271 ¶6.

[14] Letham, *The Holy Trinity*, p. 145.

unleashed sixty years of ecclesiastical and empire-wide political conflict.

Eusebius of Nicomedia (modern-day Izmit in Turkey) took up Arius's theology and became "the head and center of the Arian cause."[15] For the next forty years the eastern part of the Roman Empire (measured from the modern Istanbul eastward) was mainly Arian. That is true in spite of the fact that the great Council of Nicaea decided in favor of the full deity of Christ. Hundreds of bishops signed it and then twisted the language to say that Arianism really fit into the wording of Nicaea.

The Council of Nicaea (325)

Emperor Constantine had seen the sign of the cross during a decisive battle thirteen years before the Council of Nicaea and was converted to Christianity. He was concerned with the deeply divisive effect of the Arian controversy in the empire. Bishops had tremendous influence, and when they were at odds (as they were over this issue), it made the unity and harmony of the empire more fragile. Constantine's Christian advisor, Hosius, had tried to mediate the Arian conflict in Alexandria, but failed. So in 325 Constantine called the Council at Nicaea across the Bosporus from Constantinople (today's Istanbul). He pulled together, according to tradition,[16] 318 bishops plus other attenders like Arius and

---

[15] *NPNF*, 4:xvi.

[16] Archibald Robertson estimates the bishops at something over 250, and attributes the number 318 to the symbolic significance it had. "According to Athanasius, who again, toward the end of his life (*ad Afr.* 2) acquiesces in the precise figure 318 (Gen xiv. 14; the Greek numeral τιη combines the Cross [τ] with the initial letters of the Sacred Name [ιη]) which a later generation adopted (it first occurs in the alleged Coptic acts of the Council of Alexandria, 362, then in the Letter of Liberius to the bishops of Asia in 365), on grounds perhaps symbolical rather than historical. *NPNF*, 4:xvii n. 1.

Athanasius, neither of whom was a bishop. He fixed the order of the council and enforced its decisions with civil penalties.

The Council lasted from May through August and ended with a statement of orthodoxy that has defined Christianity to this day. The wording today that we call the Nicene Creed is really the slightly altered language of the Council of Constantinople in 381. But the decisive work was done in 325. The anathema at the end of the Creed of Nicaea shows most clearly what the issue was. The original Creed of Nicaea was written in Greek, but here it is in English:

> We believe in one God, the Father Almighty, Maker of all things visible, and invisible.
>
> And in one Lord Jesus Christ, the Son of God, begotten of the Father the only-begotten, that is, of the essence of the Father (ἐκ τῆς οὐσίας τοῦ πατρὸς), God of God (Θεὸν ἐκ Θεοῦ), and Light of Light (καὶ φῶς ἐκ φωτὸς), very God of very God (Θεὸν ἀληθινὸν ἐκ Θεου ἀληθινοῦ), begotten, not made (γεννηθέντα οὐ ποιηθέντα), being of one substance with the Father (ὁμοούσιον τῷ πατρὶ); by whom all things were made in heaven and on earth; who for us men, and for our salvation, came down and was incarnate and was made man; he suffered, and the third day he rose again, ascended into heaven; from thence he cometh to judge the quick and the dead.
>
> And in the Holy Ghost.
>
> And those who say: there was a time when he was not; and: he was not before he was made; and: he was made out of nothing, or out of another substance or thing (ἢ ἐξ ἑτέρας ὑποστάσεως ἢ οὐσίας), or the Son of God is created, or changeable, or alterable; they are condemned by the holy catholic and apostolic Church.

The key phrase, ὁμοούσιον τῷ πατρὶ (one being with the Father) was added later due to the insistence of the emperor. It made the issue crystal-clear. The Son of God could not have been created, because he did not have merely a *similar* being to the Father (ὁμοιούσιον τῷ πατρὶ), but was of the very being of the Father (ὁμοούσιον τῷ πατρὶ). He was not brought into existence with similar being, but was eternally one with divine being.

Astonishingly all but two bishops signed the creed, some, as Robertson says, "with total duplicity."[17] Bishops Secundus and Theonas, along with Arius (who was not a bishop), were sent into exile. Eusebius of Nicomedia squeaked by with what he called a "mental reservation" and within four years would persuade the emperor that Arius held substantially to the Creed of Nicaea—which was pure politics.[18]

When Athanasius's mentor, Alexander, Bishop of Alexandria, died on April 17, 328, three years after the Council of Nicaea, the mantel of Egypt and of the cause of orthodoxy fell to Athanasius. He was ordained as Bishop on June 8 that year. This bishopric was the second in Christendom after Rome. It had jurisdiction over all the bishops of Egypt and Libya. Under Athanasius Arianism died out entirely in Egypt. And from Egypt Athanasius wielded his empire-wide influence in the battle for the deity of Christ.

---

[17] *NPNF*, 4:xx.

[18] Ibid., p. xx. "In 329 we find Eusebius once more in high favor with Constantine, discharging his episcopal functions, persuading Constantine that he and Arius held substantially the Creed of Nicaea."

Athanasius, the Desert Monks, and Antony

We've passed over one crucial and decisive event in his role as Alexander's assistant. He made a visit with Alexander to the Thebaid, the desert district in southern Egypt where he came in contact with the early desert monks, the ascetics who lived lives of celibacy, solitude, discipline, prayer, simplicity, and service to the poor. Athanasius was deeply affected by this visit and was "set on fire by the holiness of their lives."[19]

For the rest of his life there was an unusual bond between the city bishop and the desert monks. They held him in awe, and he admired them and blessed them. Robinson says, "He treats . . . the monks as equals or superiors, begging them to correct and alter anything amiss in his writings."[20] The relationship became a matter of life and death because when Athanasius was driven out of his office by the forces of the empire, there was one group he knew he could trust with his protection. "The solitaries of the desert, to a man, would be faithful to Athanasius during the years of trial."[21]

One in particular captured Athanasius's attention, affection, and admiration: Antony. He was born in 251. At twenty he sold all his possessions and moved to the desert but served the poor nearby. At thirty-five he withdrew for twenty years into total solitude, and no one knew if he was alive or dead. Then at fifty-five he returned and ministered to the monks and the people who came to him for prayer and counsel in the desert until he died at 105. Athanasius wrote the biography of Antony. This was

---

[19] F. A. Forbes, *Saint Athanasius* (1919; reprint: Rockford, IL: Tan Books and Publishers, 1989), p. 8.
[20] *NPNF*, 4:lxvii.
[21] Forbes, *Saint Athanasius*, p. 36.

Athanasius's ideal, the combination of solitude and compassion for the poor based on rock-solid orthodoxy.

Antony made one rare appearance in Alexandria that we hear about, namely, to dispel the rumor that the desert monks were on the Arian side. He denounced Arianism "as the worst of heresies, and was solemnly escorted out of town by the bishop [Athanasius] in person."[22] Orthodoxy, rigorous asceticism for the sake of purity, and compassion for the poor—these were the virtues Athanasius loved in Antony and the monks. And he believed their lives were just as strong an argument for orthodox Christology as his books were.

> Now these arguments of ours do not amount merely to words, but have in actual experience a witness to their truth. For let him that will, go up and behold the proof of virtue in the virgins of Christ and in the young men that practice holy chastity, and the assurance of immortality in so great a band of His martyrs.[23]

Athanasius's biography of Antony is significant for another reason. It was translated from Greek to Latin and found its way into the hands of Ponticianus, a friend of St. Augustine, some time after 380. Ponticianus told St. Augustine the story of Antony. As he spoke, Augustine says, he was "violently overcome by a fearful sense of shame." This led to Augustine's final struggles in the garden in Milan and his eventual conversion. "Athanasius' purpose in writing Antony's *Life* had gained its greatest success:

[22] *NPNF*, 4:xlii. (July 27, 338).
[23] Ibid., p. 62.

Augustine would become the most influential theologian in the church for the next 1,000 years."[24]

Athanasius Embroiled in Controversy

Within two years after taking office as Bishop of Alexandria, Athanasius became the flash point of controversy. Most of the bishops who had signed the Creed of Nicaea did not like calling people heretics, even if they disagreed with this basic affirmation of Christ's deity. They wanted to get rid of Athanasius and his passion for this cause. Athanasius was accused of levying illegal taxes. There were accusations that he was too young when ordained, that he used magic, that he subsidized treasonable persons, and more. Constantine did not like Athanasius's hard line either and called him to Rome in 331 to face the charges the bishops were bringing. The facts acquitted him, but his defense of the Nicene formulation of Christ's deity was increasingly in the minority.

The First Exile of Athanasius (336-338)

Finally his enemies resorted to intrigue. They bribed Arsenius, a bishop in Hypsele (on the Nile in southern Egypt), to disappear so that the rumor could be started that Athanasius had arranged his murder and cut off one of his hands to use for magic. Constantine was told and asked for a trial to be held in Tyre. Meanwhile one of Athanasius's trusted deacons had found Arsenius hiding in a monastery and had taken him captive and brought him secretly to Tyre.

---

[24] David Wright, "The Life Changing 'Life of Antony,'" in *Christian History* 28 (1999), p. 17.

At the trial the accusers produced a human hand to confirm the indictment. But Athanasius was ready. "Did you know Arsenius personally?" he asked. "Yes" was the eager reply from many sides. So Arsenius was ushered in alive, wrapped up in a cloak. When he was revealed to them, they were surprised but demanded an explanation of how he had lost his hand. Athanasius turned up his cloak and showed that one hand at least was there. There was a moment of suspense, artfully managed by Athanasius. Then the other hand was exposed, and the accusers were requested to point out whence the third had been cut off.[25]

As clear as this seemed, Athanasius was condemned at this Council and fled in a boat with four bishops and came to Constantinople. The accusers threw aside the Arsenius indictment and created another with false witnesses: Athanasius had tried to starve Constantine's capitol by preventing wheat shipments from Alexandria. That was too much for Constantine, and even without condemning evidence he ordered Athanasius banished to Treveri (Trier, near today's Luxembourg). Athanasius left for exile on February 8, 336.

Constantine died the next year, and the empire was divided among his three sons, Constantius (taking the East), Constans (taking Italy and Illyricum), and Constantine II (taking the Gauls and Africa). One of Constantine II's first acts was to restore Athanasius to his office in Alexandria on November 23, 327.

---

[25] *NPNF*, 4:xl.

The Second Exile of Athanasius (339-346)

Two years later Eusebius, the leader of the Arians, had persuaded Constantius to get rid of Athanasius. He took the ecclesiastical power into his hands, declared Gregory the bishop of Alexandria, put his own secular governor in charge of the city, and used force to take the bishop's quarters and the churches. Athanasius was forced to leave the city to spare more bloodshed.

This was the beginning of his second exile—the longest time away from his flock. He left on April 16, 339, and didn't return until October 21, 346, over seven years in exile. Constantine's other two sons supported Athanasius and called the Council of Sardica (now Sophia in Bulgaria), which vindicated him in August 343. But it took three years until the political factors fell into place for his return. Constans threatened Constantius with war if he did not reinstate Athanasius. In the meantime the Arians had fallen out of favor with Constantius and the substitute bishop Gregory had died. So Athanasius was restored to his people with rejoicing after seven years away (346).

During the following season of peace Alexandria and the surrounding districts seemed to have experienced something of a revival, with a strong ascetic flavor. Athanasius wrote:

> How many unmarried women, who were before ready to enter upon marriage, now remained virgins to Christ![26]

---

[26] It is partly paradoxical that Athanasius, the great defender of the incarnation and of the honor God paid to the physical world by taking it on himself, would also be such a strong defender of celibacy as a great virtue. In fact, he sees the incarnation not so much an endorsement of the good of marriage as an empowerment to abstain from the imperfect sexual impulses that inevitably accompany marriage. "Let him that will, go up and behold the proof of virtue in the virgins of Christ and in the young men that practice holy chastity, and the assurance of immortality in so great a band of His martyrs" (*NPNF*, 4:62) "Is this, then, a slight proof of the weakness of death? Or is it a slight demonstration of the victory won over him by the Savior, when the youths and young maidens that are in Christ despise this life and *practice to*

How many young men, seeing the examples of others, embraced the monastic life! . . . How many widows and how many orphans, who were before hungry and naked, now through the great zeal of the people, were no longer hungry, and went forth clothed! In a word, so great was their emulation in virtue, that you would have thought every family and every house a Church, by reason of the goodness of its inmates, and the prayers which were offered to God. And in the Churches there was a profound and wonderful peace, while the Bishops wrote from all quarters, and received from Athanasius the customary letters of peace.[27]

The Third Exile of Athanasius (356-362)

On January 18, 350, Constans was murdered. This freed Constantius to solidify his power and to attack Athanasius and the Nicene theology unopposed. The people of Alexandria held off one armed assault on the city by the emperor's secretary Diogenes in 355, but the next year Constantius sent Syrianus, his military commander, to exert the emperor's control in Alexandria.

On Thursday night, Feb. 8 [356], Athanasius was presiding at a crowded service of preparation for a Communion on the following morning . . . in the Church of Theonas . . . the largest in the city. Suddenly the church was surrounded and the doors broken in, and just after midnight Syrianus . . . "entered with an infinite force of

---

die?" (*NPNF*, 4:51). The ascetic influence of Origen is seen here (*NPNF*, 4:xv). Thus Athanasius, with most Christians of his day, saw the body not only as a gift for experiencing God's creation, but as a fallen hindrance to rising to intellectual and spiritual enjoyment of God. For a different assessment of the function of creation in the spiritual life see John Piper, "How to Wield the World in the Fight for Joy: Using All Five Senses to See the Glory of God," in *When I Don't Desire God: How to Fight for Joy* (Wheaton, IL: Crossway Books, 2004), pp. 175-208.
[27] Ibid., 4:278.

soldiers." Athanasius . . . calmly took his seat upon the
throne (in the recess of the apse), and ordered the deacon to begin the 136th psalm, the people responding at
each verse "for His mercy endureth for ever." Meanwhile
the soldiers crowded up to the chancel, and in spite of
entreaties the bishop refused to escape until the congregation were in safety. He ordered the prayers to proceed,
and only at the last moment a crowd of monks and clergy
seized the Archbishop and managed to convey him in
the confusion out of the church in a half-fainting state . . .
but thankful that he had been able to secure the escape
of his people before his own. . . . From that moment
Athanasius was lost to public view for "six years and
fourteen days."[28]

He had spared his people briefly. But in June the hostility against
the supporters of Athanasius were attacked with a viciousness
unlike anything before.

In the early hours of Thursday, June 13 [356], after a service (which had begun overnight . . .), just as all the congregation except a few women had left, the church of
Theonas was stormed and violences perpetrated which left
far behind anything that Syrianus had done. Women were
murdered, the church wrecked and polluted with the very
worst orgies of heathenism, houses and even tombs were
ransacked throughout the city and suburbs on pretence
of "seeking for Athanasius."[29]

The secular authorities forced a new bishop on the people. It
proved to be a disaster. Bishop George instigated violent persecu-

---

[28] Ibid., p. l.
[29] Ibid., p. lii.

tion of any who sided with Athanasius and did not support the Arian cause. Many were killed and others banished. At last, in December 361, the people's patience was exhausted, and George was lynched.

Such was the mingling of secular and ecclesiastical forces in those days. But at the darkest hour for Athanasius and for the cause of orthodoxy, the dawn was about to break. This third exile proved to be the most fruitful. Protected by an absolutely faithful army of desert monks, no one could find him, and he produced his most significant written works: *The Arian History*, the four *Tracts Against Arians*, the four dogmatic letters *To Serapion*, and *On the Councils of Ariminum and Seleucia*.

This last work was a response to the two councils called by Constantius in 359 to settle the conflict between the Arians and the supporters of Nicaea. Four hundred bishops assembled in Ariminum in Italy, and 160 assembled in Seleucia in Asian Minor. The aim was a unifying creed for Christianity. The upshot of these councils was a compromise, sometimes called semi-Arian, that said the Son is "like the Father" but did not say how. It basically avoided the issue. For Athanasius this was totally unacceptable. The nature of Christ was too important to obscure with vague language.

The Triumph of God's Fugitive

It is one of the typical ironies of God's providence that the triumph over Arianism would happen largely through the ministry of a fugitive living and writing within inches of his death. Here is the way Archibald Robertson described the triumph of the third exile:

The third exile of Athanasius marks the summit of his

achievement. Its commencement is the triumph, its conclusion the collapse of Arianism. It is true that after the
death of Constantius [November 3, 361] the battle went
on with variations of fortune for twenty years, mostly
under the reign of an ardently Arian Emperor [Valens]
(364-378). But by 362 the utter lack of inner coherence
in the Arian ranks was manifest to all; the issue of the
fight might be postponed by circumstances but could not
be in doubt. The break-up of the Arian power was due to
its own lack of reality: as soon as it had a free hand, it
began to go to pieces. But the watchful eye of Athanasius
followed each step in the process from his hiding-place,
and the event was greatly due to his powerful personality
and ready pen, knowing whom to overwhelm and whom
to conciliate, where to strike and where to spare. This
period then of forced abstention from affairs was the most
stirring in spiritual and literary activity in the whole life
of Athanasius. It produced more than half of . . . his entire
extant works. . . . Let it be noted once for all how completely the amazing power wielded by the wandering fugitive was based upon the devoted fidelity of Egypt to its
pastor. Towns and villages, deserts and monasteries, the
very tombs were scoured by the Imperial inquisitors in
the search for Athanasius; but all in vain; not once do we
hear of any suspicion of betrayal. The work of the golden
decade [the period of revival before the third exile] was
bearing its fruit.[30]

Athanasius returned to Alexandria on February 21, 362 by another
irony. The new and openly pagan emperor, Julian, reversed all the
banishments of Constantius. The favor lasted only eight months.
But during these months Athanasius called a Synod at Alexandria

---

[30] Ibid., p. li.

and gave a more formal consolidation and reconciliation to the gains he had accomplished in the last six years of his writing. It had a tremendous impact on the growing consensus of the church in favor of Nicene orthodoxy. Jerome says that this synod "snatched the whole world from the jaws of Satan."[31] And Robertson calls it "the crown of the career of Athanasius."[32] The rallying point that it gave for orthodoxy in 362 enabled the reuniting forces of Eastern Christendom to withstand the political Arianism under Emperor Valens, who reigned from 364 to 378.

The Fourth Exile of Athanasius (362-364)

But in October 362 Athanasius was again driven from his office by Julian's wrath when he realized that Athanasius took his Christianity seriously enough to reject the pagan gods. Again he spent the next fifteen months among the desert monks. The story goes that he was freed to return by a prophecy by one of the monks that Julian had that very day fallen in battle in Persia. It proved true, and Athanasius was restored to his ministry on February 14, 364.

The Fifth Exile of Athanasius (365-366)

A year and a half later Emperor Valens ordered that all the bishops earlier expelled under Julian should be removed once again by the civil authorities. On October 5, 365 the Roman Prefect broke into the church in Alexandria and searched the apartments of

---

[31] Ibid., p. lviii.
[32] Ibid.

the clergy, but the sixty-seven-year-old Athanasius had been warned and escaped one last time—his fifth exile. It was short because a dangerous revolt led by Procopius had to be put down by Valens; so he judged it was not time to allow popular discontent to smolder in Athanasius-loving Alexandria. Athanasius was brought back on February 1, 366.

He spent the last years of his life fulfilling his calling as a pastor and overseer of pastors. He carried on extensive correspondence and gave great encouragement and support to the cause of orthodoxy around the empire. He died on May 2, 373.

What then may we learn about the sacred calling of controversy from the life of Athanasius?

1. Defending and explaining doctrine is for the sake of the gospel and our everlasting joy.

When Athanasius was driven into his third exile, he wrote an open letter, "To the Bishops of Egypt." In it he referred to the martyrs who had died defending the deity of Christ. Then he said, "Wherefore . . . considering that *this struggle is for our all* . . . let us also make it our earnest care and aim to guard what we have received."[33] "The Arian controversy was to him no battle for ecclesiastical power, nor for theological triumph. It was a religious crisis involving the reality of revelation and redemption."[34] He said in essence, "We are contending for our all."

What was at stake was everything. Oh, how thankful we should be that Athanasius saw things so clearly. The incarnation has to do with the gospel. It has to do with salvation. It has to do with whether there is any hope or eternal life. The creed that

---

[33] Ibid., p. 234.
[34] Ibid., p. lxvii.

Athanasius helped craft, and that he embraced and spent his life defending and explaining, says this plainly:

> We believe . . . in one Lord Jesus Christ, the Son of God, begotten of the Father . . . very God of very God . . . being of one substance with the Father . . . *who for us men, and for our salvation, came down and was incarnate* and was made man; he suffered, and the third day he rose again. . . .

In other words, the deity of the incarnate Son of God is essential for the truth and validity of the gospel of our salvation. There is no salvation if Jesus Christ is not God. It's true that Athanasius deals with salvation mainly in terms of restoring the image of God in man by Christ's taking human nature into union with the divine nature.[35] But Athanasius does not emphasize this to the exclusion of the death of Christ and the atonement. You hear both of these in this passage from *On the Incarnation of the Word*:

> For the Word, perceiving that no otherwise could the corruption of men be undone save by death as a necessary condition, while it was impossible for the Word to suffer death, being immortal, and Son of the Father; to this end He takes to Himself a body capable of death, that it, by partaking of the Word Who is above all, might be worthy to die in the stead of all, and might, because of the Word which was come to dwell in it, remain incorruptible, and that thenceforth corruption might be stayed from all by the Grace of the Resurrection. Whence, by offering unto death

---

[35] I think Robert Letham's judgment is too sweeping when he says, "For Athanasius the decisive fulcrum is the Incarnation. As a result, the Cross has diminished significance. [R. P. C.] Hanson likens his theory of salvation to a sacred blood transfusion that almost does away with a doctrine of the Atonement. Athanasius lacks reasons why Christ should have died. For him, corruption consists in fallenness, rather than in sin." Letham, *The Holy Trinity*, p. 133. More balanced and fair is the observation of Archibald Robertson: "Athanasius felt . . . the supremacy of the Cross as the purpose of the Savior's coming, but he does not in fact give to it the central place in his system of thought which it occupies in his instincts" (*NPNF*, 4:lxix).

the body He Himself had taken, as an offering and sacrifice free from any stain, straightway He put away death
from all His peers by the offering of an equivalent. For
being over all, the Word of God naturally by offering His
own temple and corporeal instrument for the life of all
satisfied the debt by His death. And thus He, the incorruptible Son of God, being conjoined with all by a like
nature, naturally clothed all with incorruption, by the
promise of the resurrection.[36]

Substitutionary Atonement for Our Debt

Yes, Christ was incarnate that "the corruption of men be
undone," and that the "corruption might be stayed." But the
human condition is not viewed only as a physical problem of
corrupt nature. It is also viewed as a moral shortfall that creates
a "debt" before God. Thus a substitutionary death is required. No
man could pay this debt. Only a God-man could pay it. This is
seen even more clearly when Athanasius, in commenting on Luke
10:22, speaks of Christ's taking the curse of God in our place:

> For man, being in Him, was quickened: for this was why
> the Word was united to man, namely, that against man
> the curse might no longer prevail. This is the reason why
> they record the request made on behalf of mankind in the
> seventy-first Psalm [sic]: 'Give the King Thy judgment, O
> God' (Ps. lxxii. I): asking that both the judgment of death
> which hung over us may be delivered to the Son, and that
> He may then, by dying for us, abolish it for us in Himself.
> This was what He signified, saying Himself, in the eighty-
> seventh Psalm [sic]: 'Thine indignation lieth hard upon me'

---

[36] *NPNF* 4:40-41.

(Ps. lxxxviii. 7). For He bore the indignation which lay upon us, as also He says in the hundred and thirty-seventh [*sic*]: 'Lord, Thou shalt do vengeance for me' (Ps. cxxxviii. 8, LXX.).[37]

Beyond merely mentioning the substitutionary sacrifice of Christ, Athanasius, in at least one place, refers to the wrath-bearing substitutionary sacrifice as the "especial cause" of the incarnation to rescue us from sin.

Since it was necessary also that the debt owing from all should be paid again: for, as I have already said, it was owing that all should die, for which *especial cause*, indeed, He came among us: to this intent, after the proofs of His Godhead from His works, He next offered up His sacrifice also on behalf of all, yielding His Temple to death in the stead of all, in order firstly to make men quit and free of their old trespass, and further to show Himself more powerful even than death, displaying His own body incorruptible, as first-fruits of the resurrection of all. (Italics added.)[38]

Athanasius is willing to make the death of Christ for our debt, owing to our trespasses, the "special cause" of the incarnation. But he returns quickly to his more common way of seeing things, namely, restoration of the image of God.

We may admit that Athanasius did not see the fullness of what Christ achieved on the cross in terms of law and guilt and justification. But what he saw we may be blind to. The implications of the incarnation are vast, and one reads Athanasius with the sense that we are paupers in our perception of what he saw. However lopsided

---

[37] Ibid., p. 88.
[38] Ibid., p. 47

his view of the cross may have been, he saw clearly that the incarnation of the divine Son of God was essential. Without it the gospel is lost. There are doctrines in the Bible that are worth dying for and living for. They are the ground of our life. They are the heart of our worship. The divine and human nature of Christ in one person is one of those doctrines. He was contending for our all.

2. Joyful courage is the calling of a faithful shepherd.

Athanasius stared down murderous intruders into his church. He stood before emperors who could have killed him as easily as exiling him. He risked the wrath of parents and other clergy by consciously training young people to give their all for Christ, including martyrdom. He celebrated the fruit of his ministry with these words: "in youth they are self-restrained, in temptations endure, in labors persevere, when insulted are patient, when robbed make light of it: and, wonderful as it is, they despise even death and become martyrs of Christ"[39]—martyrs not who kill as they die, but who love as they die.

Athanasius *contra mundum* should inspire every pastor to stand his ground meekly and humbly and courageously whenever a biblical truth is at stake. But be sure that you always outrejoice your adversaries. If something is worth fighting for, it is worth rejoicing over. And the joy is essential in the battle, for nothing is worth fighting for that will not increase our everlasting joy in God.

Courage in conflict must mingle with joy in Christ. This is what Athanasius loved about Antony and what he sought to be himself. This was part of his battle strategy with his adversaries:

---

[39] Ibid., p. 65.

> Let us be *courageous* and *rejoice* always. . . . Let us con-
> sider and lay to heart that while the Lord is with us, our
> foes can do us no hurt. . . . But if they see us *rejoicing in the*
> *Lord*, contemplating the bliss of the future, mindful of
> the Lord, deeming all things in His hand . . . —they are dis-
> comfited and turned backwards.[40]

So, Athanasius would have us learn from his life and the life of
his heroes this lesson: even if at times it may feel as though we
are alone *contra mundum*, let us stand courageous and out-rejoice
our adversaries.

**3. Loving Christ includes loving true propositions about
Christ.**

What was clear to Athanasius was that propositions about
Christ carried convictions that could send you to heaven or to hell.
Propositions like "There was a time when the Son of God was
not," and "He was not before he was made," and "the Son of God
is created" were damnable. If they were spread abroad and
believed, they would damn the souls who embraced them. And
therefore Athanasius labored with all his might to formulate
propositions that would conform to reality and lead the soul to
faith and worship and heaven.

I believe Athanasius would have abominated, with tears, the
contemporary call for "depropositionalizing" that we hear among
many of the so-called "reformists" and "the emerging church,"
"younger evangelicals," "postfundamentalists," "postfounda-
tionalists," "postpropositionalists," and "postevangelicals."[41] I

---

[40] Ibid., p. 207.
[41] See the critical interaction with these movements in Millard J. Erickson, Paul Kjoss Helseth,
Justin Taylor, eds., *Reclaiming the Center: Confronting Evangelical Accommodation in
Postmodern Times* (Wheaton, IL: Crossway Books, 2004).

think he would have said, "Our young people in Alexandria die for the truth of propositions about Christ. What do your young people die for?" And if the answer came back, "We die for Christ, not propositions about Christ," I think he would have said, "That's what the heretic Arius said. So which Christ will you die for?" To answer that question requires propositions about him. To refuse to answer implies that it doesn't matter what we believe or die for as long as it has the label *Christ* attached to it.

Athanasius would have grieved over sentences like "It is Christ who unites us; it is doctrine that divides." And sentences like: "We should ask, Whom do you trust? rather than what do you believe?"[42] He would have grieved because he knew this is the very tactic used by the Arian bishops to cover the councils with fog so that the word *Christ* could mean anything. Those who talk like this—"Christ unites, doctrine divides"—have simply replaced propositions about Christ with the word *Christ*. It carries no meaning until one says something about him. They think they have done something profound and fresh, when they call us away from the propositions of doctrine to the word *Christ*. In fact they have done something very old and worn and deadly.

This leads to a related lesson . . .

4. The truth of biblical language must be vigorously protected with non-biblical language.

Bible language can be used to affirm falsehood. Athanasius's experience has proved to be illuminating and helpful in dealing with this fact. Over the years I have seen this misuse of the Bible especially in liberally minded baptistic and pietistic traditions.

---

[42] These sentences are from E. Stanley Jones, *The Christ of the Indian Road* (New York: Abingdon, 1925), pp. 155-157. I cite this older book because it is being used with enthusiasm by some today to buttress a vision that beclouds the importance of doctrine.

They use the slogan, "the Bible is our only creed." But in refusing to let explanatory, confessional language clarify what the Bible means, the slogan can be used as a cloak to conceal the fact that Bible language is being used to affirm what is not biblical. This is what Athanasius encountered so insidiously at the Council of Nicaea. The Arians affirmed biblical sentences while denying biblical meaning. Listen to this description of the proceedings:

> The Alexandrians . . . confronted the Arians with the traditional Scriptural phrases which appeared to leave no doubt as to the eternal Godhead of the Son. But to their surprise they were met with perfect acquiescence. Only as each test was propounded, it was observed that the suspected party whispered and gesticulated to one another, evidently hinting that each could be safely accepted, since it admitted of evasion. If their assent was asked to the formula "like to the Father in all things," it was given with the reservation that man as such is "the image and glory of God." The "power of God" elicited the whispered explanation that the host of Israel was spoken of as δυναμις κυριου, and that even the locust and caterpillar are called the "power of God." The "eternity" of the Son was countered by the text, "We that live are always" (2 Corinthians 4:11)! The fathers were baffled, and the test of ομοουσιον, with which the minority had been ready from the first, was being forced upon the majority by the evasions of the Arians.[43]

R. P. C. Hanson explained the process like this: "Theologians of the Christian Church were slowly driven to a realization that the deepest questions which face Christianity cannot be answered in purely biblical language, *because the questions are about the*

---

[43] *NPNF*, 4:xvix.

meaning of biblical language itself."[44] The Arians railed against the unbiblical language being forced on them. They tried to seize the biblical high ground and claim to be the truly biblical people— the pietists, the simple Bible-believers—because they wanted to stay with biblical language only—and by it smuggle in their non-biblical meanings.

But Athanasius saw through this "postmodern," "post-conservative," "post-propositional" strategy and saved for us not just Bible words, but Bible truth. May God grant us the discernment of Athanasius for our day. Very precious things are at stake.[45]

5. A widespread and long-held doctrinal difference among Christians does not mean that the difference is insignificant or that we should not seek to persuade toward the truth and seek agreement.

What if someone had said to Athanasius, "Athanasius, people have disagreed on this issue of Christ's deity for three hundred years, and there has never been an official position taken in the church to establish one side as orthodox and the other as heresy. So who do you think you are? Half the bishops in the world [an understatement] disagree with you, and they read the same Bible you do. So stop fighting this battle and let different views exist side by side."

We may thank God that Athanasius did not think that way. He did not regard the amount of time that has elapsed or the num-

---

[44] Hanson, *The Search for the Christian Doctrine of God*, p. xxi.

[45] Another way that Athanasius and the orthodox bishops at Nicaea protected the truth was to include denials as well as affirmations. In their case they were called anathemas. The point here is this: When mistaken teachers are looking for a way to have their views accepted in the mainstream, they are often willing to agree with affirmations and give them a different meaning. Or sometimes the affirmations are broad and general and so do not make clear what is being excluded as false. But if a denial is included, which explicitly names what is being rejected as false, then the mistaken person cannot as easily weasel around the denial. For example, an open theist may affirm the statement "We believe in the full omniscience of God." But he would have a difficult time making the denial, "We deny that God is ignorant of anything that shall come to pass."

ber of Christians who disagreed to determine which doctrines are important and which we should strive to teach and spread and make normative in the church.

And so today we should not conclude that the absence of consensus in the church means doctrinal stalemate or doctrinal insignificance. God may be pleased to give the blessing of unity on some crucial areas of doctrine that are not yet resolved in the Christian church. I think, for example of the issue of manhood and womanhood, the issue of justification by faith, the issue of how the death of Christ saves sinners, and the issue of the sovereignty of God's grace in converting the soul. I don't think we should assume that, because much time has gone by and many people disagree, it must always be this way. Who knows but that, by God's amazing grace, wrong views on these things could become as marginal as the Arianism of the Jehovah's Witnesses is today. I don't mean that all these issues are as essential as the deity of Christ, but only that a much greater consensus may be reached on the true interpretation of Scripture than is often thought. I think that would be a good thing for the church and the world and the glory of Christ.

6. Pastors should not aim to preach only in categories of thought that can be readily understood by this generation. Rather we should also aim at creating biblical categories of thought that are not present.

Another way to put it is to use the terminology of Andrew Walls: Don't embrace the indigenous principle of Christianity at the expense of the pilgrim principle.[46] The indigenous principle

---

[46] Andrew Walls, *Missionary Movement in Christian History* (Mary Knoll, NY: Orbis, 2001), pp. 7-9.

says, "I have become all things to all people, that by all means I might save some" (1 Corinthians 9:22). The pilgrim principle says, "Do not be conformed to this world, but be transformed by the renewal of your mind" (Romans 12:2).

Some of the most crucial and precious truths of the Scripture are counterintuitive to the fallen human mind. They don't fit easily into our sin-soaked heads. The orthodox understanding of the Trinity is one of those. If the indigenous principle had triumphed in the fourth century, we might all be Arians. It is far easier for the human mind to say that the Son of God, like all other sons, once was not, and then came into being, than it is to say that he has always been God with the Father, and there is only one God. But the Bible will not let its message be fitted into the categories we bring with our fallen, finite minds. It presses us relentlessly to create new categories of thought to contain the mysteries of the gospel.

The Danger of Adapting to the "Seekers"

Archibald Robertson points out that with the conversion of Constantine and the Edict of Milan (313), which gave legal status to Christianity, "the inevitable influx of heathen into the Church, now that the empire had become Christian, brought with it multitudes to whom Arianism was a more intelligible creed than that of Nicaea."[47] And if you want to grow a church, the temptation is to give the people what they already have categories to understand and enjoy. But once that church is grown, it thinks so much

---

[47] NPNF, 4:xxxv.

like the world that the difference is not decisive. The radical, biblical gospel is blunted, and the glory of Christ is obscured.

Rather, alongside the indigenous principle of accommodation and contextualization, Athanasius would plead with us to have a deep commitment to the pilgrim principle of confrontation and transformation—and brain-boggling, mind-altering, recategorization of the way people think about reality.

And we must not treat these two principles as merely sequential. They start and continue together. We must not assume that the first and basic truths of Christianity fit into the fallen mind of unbelievers, and that later we transform their minds with more advanced truths. That's not the case. From the very beginning, we are speaking to them God-centered, Christ-exalting truths that shatter fallen, human categories of thought. We must not shy away from this. We must do all we can to advance it and to help people, by the grace of God, to see what is happening to them (the shattering of their categories) as the best news in all the world.

From the very beginning, in the most winsome way possible, we must labor to create categories like these (to mention a few):

• God rules the world of bliss and suffering and sin, right down to the roll of the dice and the fall of a bird and the driving of the nail into the hand of his Son; yet, though God wills that such sin and suffering exist, he does not sin, but is perfectly holy.

• God governs all the steps of all people, both good and bad, at all times and in all places, yet such that all are accountable before him and will bear the just consequences of his wrath if they do not believe in Christ.

• All are dead in their trespasses and sin and are not morally able to come to Christ because of their rebellion, yet they are responsible to come and will be justly punished if they don't.

• Jesus Christ is one person with two natures, divine and human, such that he upheld the world by the word of his power while living in his mother's womb.

• Sin, though committed by a finite person and in the confines of finite time, is nevertheless deserving of an infinitely long punishment because it is a sin against an infinitely worthy God.

• The death of the one God-man, Jesus Christ, so displayed and glorified the righteousness of God that God is not unrighteous to declare righteous ungodly people who simply believe in Christ.

These kinds of mind-boggling, category-shattering truths demand our best thought and our most creative labors. We must aim to speak them in a way that, by the power of God's Word and Spirit, a place for them would be created in the minds of those who hear. We must not preach only in the categories that are already present in our listeners' fallen minds, or we will betray the gospel and conceal the glory of God. Athanasius's lifelong struggle is a sobering witness to this truth.

7. Finally, we must not assume that old books, which say some startling things, are necessarily wrong, but that they may in fact have something glorious to teach us that we never dreamed.[48]

For example, Athanasius says some startling things about human deification that we would probably never say. Is that because one of us is wrong? Or is it because the language and the categories of thought that he uses are so different from ours that we have to get inside his head before we make judgments about

---

[48] See the quotes from C. S. Lewis in the Preface.

the truth of what he says? And might we discover something great by this effort to see what he saw?

For example, he says, "[The Son] was made man that we might be made God (θεοποιηθωμων)."[49] Or: "He was not man, and then became God, but He was God, and then became man, and that to deify us."[50] The issue here is whether the word "made God" or "deify" (θεοποιεω) means something unbiblical or whether it means what 2 Peter 1:4 means when it says, "that you may become partakers of the divine nature" (ἵνα γένησθε θείας κοινωνοὶ φύσεως). Athanasius explains it like this:

> John then thus writes; 'Hereby know we that we dwell in Him and He in us, because He hath given us of His Spirit. . . . And the Son is in the Father, as His own Word and Radiance; but we, apart from the Spirit, are strange and distant from God, and by the participation of the Spirit we are knit into the Godhead; so that our being in the Father is not ours, but is the Spirit's which is in us and abides in us. . . . What then is our likeness and equality to the Son? . . . The Son is in the Father in one way, and we become in Him in another, and that neither we shall ever be as He, nor is the Word as we.[51]

What becomes clear when all is taken into account is that Athanasius is pressing a reality in the Scriptures that we today usually call glorification. But he is using the terminology of 2 Peter 1:4 and Romans 8:29. "He has granted to us his precious and very great promises, so that through them you may become partakers of the divine nature." "Those whom he foreknew he also predes-

---

[49] *NPNF*, 4:65.
[50] Ibid., p. 329.
[51] Ibid., pp. 406-407.

tined to be conformed to the image of his Son, in order that he might be the firstborn among many brothers." Athanasius is pressing the destiny and the glory of being a brother of the second person of the Trinity and "sharing in his nature."[52]

Are We Created Finally to See or to Be?

And thus Athanasius raises for me in a fresh way one of the most crucial questions of all: What is the ultimate end of creation—the ultimate goal of God in creation and redemption? Is it being or seeing? Is it our being like Christ or our seeing the glory of Christ? How does Romans 8:29 ("predestined to be conformed to the image of his Son") relate to John 17:24 ("Father, I desire that they also, whom you have given me, may be with me where I am, to see my glory")? Is the beatific vision of the glory of the Son of God the aim of human creation? Or is likeness to that glory the aim of creation?

Athanasius has helped me go deeper here by unsettling me. (This is one of the great values of reading the old books.) I am inclined to stress *seeing* as the goal rather than *being*. The reason is that it seems to me that putting the stress on *seeing* the glory of Christ makes him the focus, but putting the stress on *being* like Christ makes me the focus. But Athanasius will not let me run away from the biblical texts. His language of deification forces me to think more deeply and worship more profoundly.

---

[52] "Glorification (in Western terminology), or deification (according to the East), is brought to fruition at the eschaton and lasts for eternity, and so is the final goal of salvation. . . . According to the Eastern church, the goal of salvation is to be made like God. This the Holy Spirit effects in us. It involves no blurring of the Creator-creature distinction, but rather focuses on the union and communion that we are given by God, in which we are made partakers of the divine nature (2 Peter 1:3)." Letham, *The Holy Trinity*, pp. 474, 498.

Created for Delighting in and Displaying the Glory of God

My present understanding would go like this: the ultimate end of creation is neither being nor seeing, but *delighting* and *displaying*. Delighting in and displaying "the glory of God in the face of Jesus Christ" (2 Corinthians 4:6). And the displaying happens both in the *delighting*, since we glorify most what we enjoy most, and in the *deeds* of the resurrection body that flow from this enjoyment on the new earth in the age to come. The display of God's glory will be both internal and external. It will be both spiritual and physical. We will display the glory of God by the Christ-exalting joy of our heart, and by the Christ-exalting deeds of our resurrection bodies.

How then should we speak of our future *being* and *seeing* if they are not the ultimate end? How shall we speak of "sharing God's nature" and being "conformed to his Son"? The way I would speak of our future *being* and *seeing* is this: by the Spirit of God who dwells in us, our final destiny is not self-admiration or self-exaltation, but *being* able to see the glory of God without disintegrating, and *being* able to delight in the glory of Christ with the very delight of God the Father for his own Son (John 17:26),[53] and *being* able to do visible Christ-exalting deeds that flow from this delight. So *being* like God is the ground of *seeing* God for who he is, and this seeing is the ground of *delighting in* the glory of God with the very delight of God, which then overflows with *visible displays* of God's glory.

---

[53] John 17:26, "I made known to them your name, and I will continue to make it known, that the love with which you have loved me may be in them, and I in them."

An Ever-Growing Wave of Revelation of God Through Man

In this way a wave of revelation of divine glory in the saints is set in motion that goes on and grows for all eternity. As each of us sees Christ and delights in Christ with the delight of the Father, mediated by the Spirit, we will overflow with visible actions of love and creativity on the new earth. In this way we will see the revelation of God's glory in each other's lives in ever new ways. New dimensions of the riches of the glory of God in Christ will shine forth every day from our new delights and new deeds. And these in turn will become new seeings of Christ that will elicit new delights and new doings. And so the ever-growing wave of the revelation of the riches of the glory of God will roll on forever and ever.

And we will discover that this was possible only because the infinite Son of God took on himself human nature so that we in our human nature might be united to him and display more and more of his glory. We will find in our eternal experience of glorification that God's infinite beauty took on human form so that our human form might increasingly display his infinite beauty.

I am thankful to God that I did not run away from the ancient and strange word "deification" in Athanasius. There is here "a grace the magnitude of which our minds can never fully grasp."[54] Thank you, Athanasius. Thank you, not only for pressing the meaning of 2 Peter 1:4 (partakers of the divine nature), but even more for a lifetime of exile and suffering for the glory of Christ. Thank you for not backing down when you were almost alone.

---

[54] John Calvin, quoted in Letham, *The Holy Trinity*, p. 472.

Thank you for seeing the truth so clearly and for standing firm. You were a gift of God to the church and the world. I join Parker Williamson in one final accolade to the glory of Christ:

> Athanasius set his name to the creed which expressed his belief, and for fifty years he stood unswervingly by that confession. Every argument that ingenuity could invent was used to prove it false. Bishops met together in great numbers, condemned his views, and invoked upon him the curse of God. Emperors took sides against him, banished him time and time again, and chased him from place to place, setting a reward on his head. At one time all bishops of the church were persuaded or coerced into pronouncing sentence against him, so that the phrase originated, "Athanasius against the world." But with all this pressure bearing on him, he changed his ground not one inch. His clear eye saw the truth once, and he did not permit his conscience to tamper with temptations to deny it. His loyalty to the truth made him a great power for good, and a great blessing to the churches of his own, and of all times.[55]

---

[55] Parker T. Williamson, *Standing Firm: Reclaiming Christian Faith in Times of Controversy* (Springfield, PA: PLC Publications, 1996), p. 38.

[More important than all is] a diligent endeavor to have the power of the truths professed and contended for abiding upon our hearts, that we may not contend for notions, but that we have a practical acquaintance within our own souls. When the heart is cast indeed into the mould of the doctrine that the mind embraceth—when the evidence and necessity of the truth abides in us—when not the sense of the words only is in our heads, but the sense of the thing abides in our hearts—when we have communion with God in the doctrine we contend for—then shall we be garrisoned by the grace of God against all the assaults of men.

JOHN OWEN, THE WORKS OF JOHN OWEN,
ED. WILLIAM GOOLD, VOL. XII,
(EDINBURGH: BANNER OF TRUTH, 1965), P. 52

2

COMMUNING WITH GOD IN THE THINGS FOR WHICH WE CONTEND

How John Owen Killed His Own Sin While Contending for Truth

Standing on Owen's Shoulders

Some of us stand on the shoulders of men who have stood on the shoulders of John Owen. J. I. Packer, Roger Nicole, and Sinclair Ferguson, for example, are three contemporary pillars in the house of my thinking, and each has testified publicly that John Owen is the most influential Christian writer in his life. That is amazing for a man who has been dead for over three hundred years, and who wrote in a style so difficult to read that even he saw his work as immensely demanding in his own generation.

One example of a difficult but compelling book is *The Death of Death in the Death of Christ*, probably his most famous and most influential book. It was published in 1647 when Owen was thirty-one years old. It is the fullest and probably the most persuasive book ever written on the doctrine sometimes called "limited atonement," or better called "definite atonement" or "particular redemption."

The point of the book is that when Paul says, "Christ loved *the church* and gave himself up *for her*" (Ephesians 5:25), he means that Christ really did something decisive and unique for the church when he died for her—something that is particular and sovereign, and different from what he does for people who experience his final judgment and wrath. The book argues that the particular love that Christ has for his bride is something more wonderful than the general love he has for his enemies. It is a *covenant* love. It pursues and overtakes and subdues and forgives and transforms and overcomes every resistance in the beloved. *The Death of Death* is a great and powerful book—it kept me up for many evenings several decades ago as I was trying to decide what I really believed about the third point of Calvinism (limited atonement).[1]

But back to the point: it is amazing that Owen can have such remarkable impact *today* when he has been dead over three hundred years. And it is all the more amazing when you realize that his style of writing is extremely difficult. Even he knows his work

---

[1] The claim of this doctrine is commonly misunderstood. It does not mean that not all who come to Christ can be saved. They can. Nor does it mean that John 3:16 isn't true—that "God so loved the world, that he gave his only Son, that whoever believes in him should not perish but have eternal life." Indeed the giving of the Son and his death have purchased a *bona fide* offer of salvation for all people. *Whoever* believes will not perish but have eternal life. This universal offer of the gospel purchased by the blood of Christ is not denied by the doctrine of particular redemption. Rather this doctrine asserts that, and more. It goes beyond these truths to make another biblical truth clear, namely, that in the death of Christ, God really paid the debt for all the sins of all the elect (all who would believe on him). Christ really and effectively absorbed all the wrath that was owing to his bride. He did not absorb all the wrath that would one day be poured out on those who do not believe. No sin is punished twice, once in Jesus and once in hell. The punishment of sin in the cross was "definite" or "particular." That is, it was the particular, definite, effective punishment owing to the elect—those who would believe. The blood of Christ purchased the new covenant promises (Luke 22:20). And these promises are not simply offers of salvation. They are effective causes of salvation: "I will put the fear of me in their hearts, that they may not turn from me" (Jeremiah 32:40). The power and efficacy of the atonement is greater than most Christians have seriously considered. It does not just offer salvation. It does that *and* accomplishes the propitiation of God's elect. To know yourself loved by the Christ of Calvary in a saving way is not merely to know the love of one who *offers* you life and watches to see what you will do with it, but rather one who purchases you particularly, pursues you particularly, conquers you, wakens your faith, and gives you life with him forever. This is what he bought at Calvary, not just the possibility for you to pursue him. If you want the best statement on this doctrine go to Owen himself, *The Death of Death in the Death of Christ*.

is difficult. In the Preface ("To the Reader") of *The Death of Death* Owen does what no good marketing agent would allow today. He begins like this: "READER, . . . If thou art, as many in this pretending age, *a sign or title gazer*, and comest into books as Cato into the theatre, to go out again—thou hast had thy entertainment; farewell!"[2]

Nevertheless, J. I. Packer and Roger Nicole and Sinclair Ferguson did not bid Owen farewell. They lingered. And they learned. And today all three of them say that no Christian writer has had a greater impact on them than John Owen.

Owen Saved Packer's Life

Packer says that Owen is the hero of his book *A Quest for Godliness*, a book about *The Puritan Vision of the Christian Life*. That is saying a lot, because for Packer the Puritans are the redwoods in the forest of theology.[3] And John Owen is "the greatest among the Puritan theologians." In other words, he is the tallest of the redwoods. "For solidity, profundity, massiveness and majesty in exhibiting from Scripture God's ways with sinful mankind there is no one to touch him."[4]

But Packer has a very personal reason for loving John Owen. I've heard him tell the story of the crisis he came into soon after his conversion. He was in danger in his student days of despairing under a perfectionistic teaching that did not take indwelling sin seriously. The discovery of John Owen brought him back to

---

[2] John Owen, *The Death of Death in the Death of Christ*, in *The Works of John Owen*, ed. William Goold, Vol. X (Edinburgh: Banner of Truth, 1965), p. 149.

[3] J.I. Packer, *A Quest for Godliness: The Puritan Vision of the Christian Life* (Wheaton, IL: Crossway Books, 1990), p. 11.

[4] Ibid., p. 81.

reality. "Suffice it to say," Packer recalls, "that without Owen I might well have gone off my head or got bogged down in mystical fanaticism."[5]

So Packer virtually says he owes his life, and not just his theology, to John Owen. It's not surprising then that Packer would say with regard to Owen's style that, while laborious and difficult, "the reward to be reaped from studying Owen is worth all the labour involved."[6]

Nicole Puts Owen Over Edwards

Roger Nicole, who taught at Gordon-Conwell Seminary for over forty years, said when he was at the Bethlehem Conference for Pastors that John Owen is the greatest theologian who has ever written in the English language. He paused and added, "even greater than the great Jonathan Edwards!" That really caught my attention, because others have considered Edwards peerless in America,[7] if not the English-speaking world, or even more widely.[8]

---

[5] Ibid., p. 12. The story is told more fully in John Owen, *Sin and Temptation*, abridged and edited by James M. Houston (Portland: Multnomah Press, 1983), Introduction, pp. xxv-xxix.

[6] Packer, *A Quest for Godliness*, p. 147.

[7] "Jonathan Edwards has proven to be the most influential religious thinker in American history." Douglas Sweeney, "Edwards' Legacy," Jonathan Edwards Center at Yale University web site (http://edwards.yale.edu/about-edwards/legacy/). Paul Ramsey called him "the greatest philosopher-theologian yet to grace the American scene." Perry Miller, "General Editor's Note," *The Works of Jonathan Edwards*, Vol. 1, *Freedom of the Will*, ed. Paul Ramsey (New Haven, CT: Yale University Press, 1957), p. viii.

[8] Martyn Lloyd-Jones said, "I am tempted, perhaps foolishly, to compare the Puritans to the Alps, Luther and Calvin to the Himalayas, and Jonathan Edwards to Mount Everest! He has always seemed to me the man most like the Apostle Paul." Quoted by Samuel T. Logan in the foreword to Stephen Nichols, *Jonathan Edwards: A Guided Tour of His Life and Thought* (Phillipsburg, NJ: P&R, 2001), p. 9. Other superlative descriptions of Edwards can be found in Iain Murray, *Jonathan Edwards: A New Biography* (Edinburgh: Banner of Truth, 1987), pp. xv-xvii.

Owen's Impact on a Teenager

Sinclair Ferguson wrote an entire book on Owen, *John Owen on the Christian Life*, and tells us about his debt that began, if you can believe it, when he was still a teenager:

> My personal interest in [Owen] as a teacher and theologian began in my late teenage years when I first read some of his writing. Like others, before and since, I found that they dealt with issues which contemporary evangelical literature rarely, if ever, touched. Owen's penetrating exposition opened up areas of need in my own heart, but also correspondingly profound assurances of grace in Jesus Christ. . . . Ever since those first encounters with his *Works*, I have remained in his debt. . . . To have known the pastoral ministry of John Owen during these years (albeit in written form) has been a rich privilege; to have known Owen's God an even greater one.[9]

The Atlas of Independency

Of course, the magnitude of John Owen's influence goes well beyond these three men. To Ambrose Barnes he was "the Calvin of England." To Anthony Wood, he was "the Atlas and Patriarch of Independency."[10] Charles Bridges, in *The Christian Ministry* (1830), said,

> Indeed upon the whole—for luminous exposition, and powerful defense of Scriptural doctrine—for determined enforcement of practical obligation—for skillful anatomy

---

[9] Sinclair B. Ferguson, *John Owen on the Christian Life* (Edinburgh: Banner of Truth, 1987), pp. x-xi.
[10] Both quotes are from Peter Toon, *God's Statesman: The Life and Work of John Owen* (Exeter, Devon: Paternoster, 1971), p. 173.

of the self-deceitfulness of the heart—and for a detailed and wise treatment of the diversified exercises of the Christian's heart, he stands probably unrivalled.[11]

If Nicole and Bridges are right—that John Owen is unrivaled in the English-speaking world—then Jonathan Edwards is not too far behind, and Edwards pays his respect to Owen not only by quoting him substantially in *Religious Affections*, but also by recording in his "Catalogue" of readings the recommendation of Hallyburton to his students at St. Andrews University that the writings of John Owen are to be valued "above all human writings for a true view of the mystery of the gospel."[12]

One of the reasons I linger over these tributes so long is that I want you to feel drawn not just to Owen, but to the value of having some great heroes in the Christian ministry. There are not many around today. And God wills that we have heroes. Hebrews 13:7 says, "Remember your leaders, those who spoke to you the word of God. *Consider the outcome of their way of life, and imitate their faith.*" It seems to me that the Christian leaders today who come closest to *being* heroes are the ones who *had* great heroes. I hope you have one or two, living or dead. Maybe Owen will become one. It would be a good choice.[13]

---

[11] Charles Bridges, *The Christian Ministry* (Edinburgh: Banner of Truth, 1967, originally published 1830), p. 41.

[12] Jonathan Edwards, *Religious Affections*, ed. John E. Smith (New Haven, CT: Yale University Press, 1959), p. 69. The quotes of Owen in Edwards are on pp. 250ff., 372ff.

[13] For a complete bibliography of writings by and about Owen, see www.johnowen.org. A helpful overview of Owen's theology can be found in Sinclair Ferguson's *John Owen on the Christian Life* (Edinburgh: Banner of Truth, 1987). Two significant academic works on Owen are forthcoming: Carl R Trueman, *John Owen: Scholasticism and Catholicity* (Aldershot: Ashgate, forthcoming); and Kelly M. Kapic, *Communion with God: Relations Between the Divine and the Human in the Theology of John Owen* (Grand Rapids, MI: Baker Academic, forthcoming).

How We Know of Owen's Life

Most people—even pastors and theologians—don't know much about John Owen. One of the reasons is that his writings are not popular today.[14] But another reason is that not much is known about him—at least not much about his personal life. Peter Toon, in his 1971 biography, says, "Not one of Owen's diaries has been preserved; and . . . the extant letters in which he lays bare his soul are very few, and recorded, personal reactions of others to him are brief and scarce."[15] "We have to rely on a few letters and a few remarks of others to seek to understand him as a man. And these are insufficient to probe the depths of his character. So Owen must remain hidden as it were behind a veil . . . his secret thoughts remain his own."[16]

I think this may be a little misleading because when you read the more practical works of Owen, the man shines through in a way that I think reveals the deep places of his heart. But still the details of his personal life are frustratingly few. You will see this—and perhaps share my frustration—in what follows.

What Is Puritanism?

Owen was born in England in 1616, the same year that William Shakespeare died and four years before the Pilgrims set sail for New England. This is virtually in the middle of the great Puritan century (roughly 1560 to 1660).

---

[14] The Banner of Truth Trust has caused a little renaissance of interest by publishing his collected works in twenty-three volumes (seven of them the massive *Hebrews* commentary) plus a number of abridged paperbacks. Owen's writings are also available on CD-Rom from Ages Software.

[15] Toon, *God's Statesman*, p. vii.

[16] Ibid., p. 177.

Puritanism was at heart a spiritual movement, passionately concerned with God and godliness. It began in England with William Tyndale the Bible translator, Luther's contemporary, a generation before the word "Puritan" was coined, and it continued till the latter years of the seventeenth century, some decades after "Puritan" had fallen out of use. . . . Puritanism was essentially a movement for church reform, pastoral renewal and evangelism, and spiritual revival. . . . The Puritan goal was to complete what England's Reformation began: to finish reshaping Anglican worship, to introduce effective church discipline into Anglican parishes, to establish righteousness in the political, domestic, and socio-economic fields, and to convert all Englishmen to a vigorous evangelical faith.[17]

Birth and Boyhood

Owen was born in the middle of this movement and became its greatest pastor-theologian, as the movement ended almost simultaneously with his death in 1683.[18] His father was a pastor in Stadham five miles north of Oxford. He had three brothers and a sister. In all his writings he does not mention his mother or his siblings. There is one brief reference to his father that says, "I was bred up from my infancy under the care of my father, who was a Nonconformist all his days, and a painful laborer in the vineyard of the Lord."[19]

At the age of ten he was sent to the grammar school run by Edward Sylvester in Oxford where he prepared for the univer-

---

[17] Packer, *A Quest for Godliness*, p. 28.

[18] J. I. Packer says that Puritanism developed under Elizabeth, James, and Charles and blossomed in the Interregnum (1640s and 1650s), before it withered in the dark tunnel of persecution between 1660 (Restoration) and 1689 (Toleration). *A Quest for Godliness*, p. 28ff.

[19] *Works*, XII:224.

sity. He entered Queens College, Oxford at twelve, took his Bachelor of Arts at sixteen and his M.A. three years later at nineteen. We can get a flavor of what the boy was like from the observation by Peter Toon that Owen's zeal for knowledge was so great at this time that "he often allowed himself only four hours of sleep each night. His health was affected, and in later life, when he was often on a sick-bed, he regretted these hours of rest that he had missed as a youth."[20]

Owen began his work for the B.D. but could not stand the high-church Arminianism and the formalism of Oxford, and finally dropped out to become a personal tutor and chaplain to some wealthy families near London.

Five Events That Shaped His Life

In 1642 the civil war began between Parliament and King Charles (between the high-church religion of William Laud and the Puritan religion of the Presbyterians and Independents in the House of Commons). Owen was sympathetic with Parliament against the king and Bishop Laud, and so he was pushed out of his chaplaincy and moved to London where five major events of his life happened in the next four years that stamped the rest of his life.

Owen's Conversion

The first is his conversion—or possibly the awakening of the assurance of salvation and the deepening of his personal communion with God. It is remarkable that it happened in a way

---

[20] Toon, *God's Statesman*, p. 6.

almost identical to Charles Spurgeon's conversion two centuries later. On January 6, 1850 Spurgeon was driven by a snowstorm into a Primitive Methodist Chapel where a layman stood in for the pastor and took the text from Isaiah, "Look to me and be saved, all the ends of the earth." Spurgeon looked and was saved.[21]

Owen was a convinced Calvinist with large doctrinal knowledge, but he lacked the sense of the reality of his own salvation. That sense of personal reality in all that he wrote was going to make all the difference in the world for Owen in the years to come. So what happened one Sunday in 1642 is very important.

When Owen was twenty-six years old he went with his cousin to hear the famous Presbyterian Edmund Calamy at St. Mary's Church Aldermanbury. But it turned out Calamy could not preach and a country preacher took his place. Owen's cousin wanted to leave. But something held Owen to his seat. The simple preacher took as his text Matthew 8:26, "Why are you fearful, O you of little faith?" It was God's appointed word and appointed time for Owen's awakening. His doubts and fears and worries as to whether he was truly born anew by the Holy Spirit were gone. He felt himself liberated and adopted as a Son of God. When you read the penetrating, practical works of Owen on the work of the Spirit and the nature of true communion with God, it is hard to doubt the reality of what God did on this Sunday in 1642.[22]

---

[21] Charles Spurgeon, C.H. *Spurgeon: Autobiography*, 2 vols. (Edinburgh: Banner of Truth: 1962), 1:87.
[22] Toon, *God's Statesman*, p. 12ff.

Owen's Marriage and Dying Children

The second crucial event in those early years in London was Owen's marriage to a young woman named Mary Rooke. He was married to her for thirty-one years, from 1644 to 1675. We know virtually nothing about her. But we do know one absolutely stunning fact that must have colored all of Owen's ministry for the rest of his life (he died eight years after she died). We know that she bore him eleven children, and all but one died as a child, and that one daughter died as a young adult. In other words, Owen experienced the death of eleven children and the death of his wife! That's one child born and lost on average every three years of Owen's adult life.[23]

We don't have one reference to Mary or to the children or to his pain in all his books. But just knowing that the man walked in the valley of the shadow of death most of his life gives me a clue to the depth of dealing with God that we find in his works. God has his strange and painful ways of making his ministers the kind of pastors and theologians he wants them to be.

His First Book: Displaying Arminianism

The third event in these early London years is the publishing of his first book. He had read thoroughly about the recent controversy in Holland between the Remonstrants (whom he called

---

[23] Andrew Thomson wrote, "Nearly all the information that has descended to us regarding this union [with Mary], from the earlier biographies amounts to this,—that the lady bore to him eleven children, all of whom, except one daughter, died in early youth. This only daughter became the wife of a Welsh gentleman; but the union proving unhappy, she 'returned to her kindred and to her father's house,' and soon after died of consumption." *Works*, I:xxxiii. "When she died in 1676 [Owen] remained a widower for about 18 months and married Dorothy D'Oyley. His exercises by affliction were very great in respect of his children, none of whom he much enjoyed while living, and saw them all go off the stage before him." *Works*, I:xcv.

Arminians) and the Calvinists. The Remonstrance was written in 1610, and the Calvinist response was the Synod of Dordt in 1618. In spite of all its differences Owen saw the English High Church of William Laud and the Dutch Remonstrants as essentially one in their rejection of predestination, which for Owen had become utterly crucial, especially since his conversion that he so thoroughly attributed to God.

So he published his first book in April 1643 with the polemical, preface-like title *A Display of Arminianism: being a discovery of the old Pelagian idol, free-will, with the new goddess, contingency, advancing themselves into the throne of God in heaven to the prejudice of His grace, providence and supreme dominion over the children of men.*[24] This is important not only because it set his direction as a Calvinist, but as a public, controversial writer whose whole life would be swallowed up by writing to the final month of his life in 1683.

Owen Becomes a Pastor

The fourth crucial event in these years was Owen's becoming a pastor of a small parish in Fordham, Essex, on July 16, 1643. He didn't stay long in this church. But I mention it because it set the course of his life as a pastor. He was always essentially a pastor, even when involved with administration at the University of Oxford and even when involved with the political events of his day. He was anything but a cloistered academic. All of his writing was done in the press of pastoral duties. There are points in his life where this will seem utterly amazing—that he could keep on

---

[24] This treatise is found in Volume X, *Works*.

studying and writing with the kind of involvements and burdens that he carried.

Owen Catapulted into Political Life

The fifth event of these early years in London was the invitation in 1646 to speak to the Parliament. In those days there were fast days during the year when the government asked certain pastors to preach to the House of Commons. It was a great honor. This message catapulted Owen into political affairs for the next fourteen years.

Owen came to the attention of Oliver Cromwell, the governmental leader ("Protector") in the absence of a king, and Cromwell is reputed to have said to Owen, "Sir, you are a person I must be acquainted with"; to which Owen replied, "That will be much more to my advantage than yours."[25]

Well, maybe and maybe not. With that acquaintance, Owen was thrown into the turmoil of the civil war. Cromwell made him his chaplain and carried him off to Ireland and Scotland to preach to his troops and to assess the religious situation in those countries and to give the theological justification for Cromwell's politics.

Vice Chancellor of Oxford University

Not only that, Cromwell in 1651 appointed Owen to the deanship at Christ Church College in Oxford and then the next year made

[25] *A Religious Encyclopedia*, ed. Philip Schaff (New York: The Christian Literature Co., 1888), Vol. 3, p. 1711.

him also the Vice Chancellor. He was involved with Oxford for nine years until 1660 when Charles II returned and things began to go very badly for the Puritans.

It is astonishing how Owen was able to keep on studying and writing in spite of how public and how administratively laden his life was. At Oxford, Owen was responsible for the services of worship because Christ Church was a cathedral as well as a college and he was the preacher. He was responsible for the choice of students, the appointment of chaplains, the provision of tutorial facilities, the administration of discipline, the oversight of property, the collection of rents and tithes, the gift of livings, and the care of almsmen for the church hospital. His whole aim in all his duties, Peter Toon says, was "to establish the whole life of the College on the Word of God."[26]

His life was pervaded with pressure. It is hard to imagine what kind of family life he had. And we should keep in mind that during this time his children were dying. We know that at least two sons died in the plague of 1655. When he finished his duties as Vice Chancellor he said in his closing address,

> Labors have been numberless; besides submitting to enormous expense, often when brought to the brink of death on your account, I have hated these limbs and this feeble body which was ready to desert my mind; the reproaches of the vulgar have been disregarded; the envy of others has been overcome: in these circumstances I wish you all prosperity and bid you farewell.[27]

---

[26] Toon, *God's Statesman*, p. 54.
[27] Ibid., p. 77ff.

Owen Ever Studying, Ever Writing

In spite of all this administrative pressure, and even hostility because of his commitment to godliness and to the Puritan cause, he was constantly studying and writing, probably late at night instead of sleeping. That's how concerned he was with doctrinal faithfulness to Scripture. Peter Toon lists twenty-two published works during those years. For example, he published his defense of the *Saints' Perseverance* in 1654. He saw a man named John Goodwin spreading error on this doctrine and he felt constrained, despite all his other duties, to answer him—with over six hundred pages! It fills all of Volume 11 in his *Works*. And he wasn't writing fluff that would vanish overnight. One biographer said that this book is "the most masterly vindication of the perseverance of the saints in the English tongue."[28]

During these administrative years he also wrote *Of the Mortification of Sin in Believers* (1656), *Of Communion with God* (1657), and *Of Temptation: The Nature and Power of It* (1658). What is so remarkable about these books is that they are what I would call intensely personal and in many places very sweet. So he wasn't just fighting doctrinal battles—he was fighting sin and temptation. And he wasn't just fighting—he was fostering heartfelt communion with God in the students.

Fugitive Pastor to the End

He was relieved of his duties of the Deanship in 1660 (having laid down the Vice Chancellorship in 1657). Cromwell had died

---

[28] Owen, *Works*, I:lvii.

in 1658. The monarchy with Charles II was back. The Act of Uniformity, which put two thousand Puritans out of their pulpits, was just around the corner (1662). The days ahead for Owen now were not the great political, academic days of the last fourteen years. He was now, from 1660 until his death in 1683, a kind of fugitive pastor in London.

During these years he became what some have called the "Atlas and Patriarch of Independency." He had begun his ministry as a Puritan of Presbyterian persuasion. But he became persuaded that the Congregational form of government is more biblical. He was the main spokesman for this wing of Nonconformity and wrote extensively to defend the view.[29]

A Defender of Tolerance against State Oppression

But even more significant, he was the main spokesman for *tolerance* of both Presbyterian and Episcopal forms. Even while at Oxford he had the authority to quash Anglican worship, but he allowed a group of Episcopalians to worship in rooms across from his own quarters.[30] He wrote numerous tracts and books to call for tolerance within Orthodoxy. For example, in 1667 he wrote (in *Indulgence and Toleration Considered*):

> It seems that we are some of the first who ever anywhere in the world, from the foundation of it, thought of ruining and destroying persons of the same religion with ourselves,

---

[29] *A Discourse Concerning Evangelical Love, Church Peace and Unity* (1672); *An Inquiry into the Original Nature . . . and Communion of Evangelical Churches* (1681); and the classic text, *True Nature of a Gospel Church* (1689 posthumously).
[30] *Works*, I:li.

merely upon the choice of some peculiar ways of worship in that religion.[31]

His ideas on tolerance were so significant that they had a large influence on William Penn, the Quaker and founder of Pennsylvania, who was a student of Owen. And it is significant to me as a Baptist that in 1669 he wrote, with several other pastors, a letter of concern to the governor and Congregationalists of Massachusetts pleading with them not to persecute the Baptists.[32]

Caring for His Flock, Even When Absent

During these twenty-three years after 1660 Owen was a pastor. Because of the political situation he was not always able to stay in one place and be with his people, but he seemed to carry them on his heart even when he was moving around. Near the end of his life he wrote to his flock, "Although I am absent from you in body, I am in mind and affection and spirit present with you, and in your assemblies; for I hope you will be found my crown and rejoicing in the day of the Lord."[33]

Not only that, he actively counseled and made plans for their care in his absence. He exhorted them in one letter with words that are amazingly relevant to pastoral care struggles in our churches today:

I beseech you to hear a word of advice in case the persecution increases, which it is like to do for a season. I could

[31] Toon, *God's Statesman*, p. 132.
[32] Ibid., p. 162. See the letter in Peter Toon, ed. *The Correspondence of John Owen (1616-1683)* (Cambridge: James Clarke and Co. Ltd., 1970), pp. 145-146.
[33] Toon, *God's Statesman*, p. 157.

wish that because you have no ruling elders, and your teachers cannot walk about publicly with safety, that you would appoint some among yourselves, who may continually as their occasions will admit, go up and down from house to house and apply themselves peculiarly to the weak, the tempted, the fearful, those who are ready to despond, or to halt, and to encourage them in the Lord. Choose out those unto this end who are endued with a spirit of courage and fortitude; and let them know that they are happy whom Christ will honor with His blessed work. And I desire the persons may be of this number who are faithful men, and know the state of the church; by this means you will know what is the frame of the members of the church, which will be a great direction to you, even in your prayers.[34]

Under normal circumstances Owen believed and taught that "The first and principal duty of a pastor is to feed the flock by diligent preaching of the word."[35] He pointed to Jeremiah 3:15 and the purpose of God to "give to his church pastors according to his own heart, who should feed them with knowledge and understanding." He showed that the care of preaching the gospel was committed to Peter, and in him to all true pastors of the church under the name of "feeding" (John 21:15-17). He cited Acts 6 and the apostles' decision to free themselves from all encumbrances that they may give themselves wholly to the Word and prayer. He referred to 1 Timothy 5:17—it is the pastor's duty to "labor in the word and doctrine," and to Acts 20:28 where the overseers of the flock are to feed them with the Word. Then he says,

---

[34] Toon, ed., *The Correspondence of John Owen*, p. 171.
[35] *Works*, XVI:74.

> Nor is it required only that he preach now and then at his leisure; but that he lay aside all other employments, though lawful, all other duties in the church, as unto such a constant attendance on them as would divert him from this work, that he give himself unto it. . . . Without this, no man will be able to give a comfortable account of his pastoral office at the last day.[36]

I think it would be fair to say that this is the way Owen fulfilled his charge during these years whenever the political situation allowed him.

Owen and Bunyan, the Patriarch and the Prisoner

During these last years of Owen's life some Puritans were in prison, and others, like Owen, were not. Part of the explanation was how openly they preached. Part of it was that Owen was a national figure with connections in high places. Part of it was that the persecution was not nationally uniform, but some local officials were more rigorous than others.

But whatever the explanation for Owen's freedom while others were in prison, the kind of relationship that he had in these years with John Bunyan, who spent too many of them in prison, was remarkable. One story says that King Charles II asked Owen one time why he bothered going to hear an uneducated tinker like Bunyan preach. Owen replied, "Could I possess the tinker's abilities for preaching, please your majesty, I would gladly relinquish all my learning."[37]

---

[36] *Works*, XVI:74-75.
[37] Toon, *God's Statesman*, p. 162.

One of the best illustrations of God's mercy in a frowning providence is the story of how Owen failed to help Bunyan get out of prison. Repeatedly when Bunyan was in prison Owen worked for his release with all the strings he could pull. But to no avail. But when John Bunyan came out in 1676 he brought with him a manuscript "the worth and importance of which can scarcely be comprehended"—*Pilgrim's Progress*.[38] In fact, Owen met with Bunyan and recommended his own publisher, Nathaniel Ponder. The partnership succeeded, and the book that has probably done more good than any book besides the Bible was released to the world—all because Owen failed in his good attempts to get Bunyan released.

> *Judge not the Lord by feeble sense,*
> *But trust him for his grace;*
> *Behind a smiling providence*
> *He hides a smiling face.*[39]

Buried Together

Owen died on August 24, 1683. He was buried on September 4 in Bunhill Fields, London where five years later the tinker and immortal dreamer of Bedford Jail was buried with him. It was fitting for the two to lie down together when the Congregational giant had labored so long in the cause of toleration for lowly Baptists in England and New England.

---

[38] Ibid., p. 161.
[39] William Cowper, "God Moves in a Mysterious Way."

His All-Encompassing Aim: Holiness—His Own and Others'

Let's stand back now and try to get close to the heart of what made this man tick and what made him great. Let us be inspired by this man in some deeply personal and spiritual ways. That seems to be the way he has touched people most—people like J. I. Packer and Sinclair Ferguson.

I think the words that come closest to giving us the heart and aim of his life are found in the preface to the little book *Of the Mortification of Sin in Believers*, which was based on sermons that he preached to the students and academic community at Oxford:

> I hope I may own in sincerity that my heart's desire unto God, and the chief design of my life . . . are, that mortification and universal holiness may be promoted in my own and in the hearts and ways of others, to the glory of God, that so the Gospel of our Lord and Savior Jesus Christ may be adorned in all things.[40]

"Mortification" means warfare on our own sin with a view to killing it. His book was an exposition of Romans 8:13 ("If you live according to the flesh you will die, but if by the Spirit you put to death the deeds of the body, you will live"). He paraphrased this truth in the memorable phrase, "Be killing sin or it will be killing you."[41]

That book was written in 1656. Twenty-five years later he was still sounding the same note in his preaching and writing. In 1681 he published *The Grace and Duty of Being Spiritually Minded*.

---

[40] *Works*, VI:4.
[41] Ibid., p. 9.

Sinclair Ferguson is probably right when he says, "*Everything* he wrote for his contemporaries had a practical and pastoral aim in view—the promotion of true Christian living"[42]—in other words, the mortification of sin and the advancement of holiness.

This was his burden not only for the churches but also for the university when he was there. Peter Toon says, "Owen's special emphasis was to insist that the whole academic curriculum be submerged in preaching and catechizing and prayer. He wanted the graduates of Oxford not only to be proficient in the Arts and Sciences but also to aspire after godliness."[43]

Calling Parliament to Personal Holiness

Even in his political messages—the sermons to Parliament—the theme was repeatedly personal holiness. He based this on the Old Testament pattern—"the people of Israel were at the height of their fortunes when their leaders were godly."[44] So the key issue for him was that the legislature be made up of holy people.

His concern that the gospel spread and be adorned with holiness was not just a burden for his English homeland. When he came back from Ireland in 1650 where he had seen the English forces, under Cromwell, decimate the Irish, he preached to Parliament and pleaded for another kind of warfare:

> How is it that Jesus Christ is in Ireland only as a lion staining all his garments with the blood of his enemies; and

---

[42] Ferguson, *John Owen on the Christian Life*, p. xi. Italics added. See below, n. 58.
[43] Toon, *God's Statesman*, p. 78.
[44] Ibid., p. 120.

none to hold him out as a Lamb sprinkled with his own blood to his friends? . . . Is this to deal fairly with the Lord Jesus?—call him out to do battle and then keep away his crown? God hath been faithful in doing great things for you; be faithful in this one—do your utmost for the preaching of the Gospel in Ireland.[45]

From his writings and from the testimony of others it seems fair to say that the aim of personal holiness in all of life, and the mortifying of all known sin, really was the labor not only of his teaching but of his own personal life.

The Divine Luster of All His Accomplishments

David Clarkson, his pastoral associate in the later years of Owen's ministry, gave his funeral address. In it he said:

A great light is fallen; one of eminency for holiness, learning, parts and abilities; a pastor, a scholar, a divine of the first magnitude; holiness gave a divine luster to his other accomplishments, it shined in his whole course, and was diffused through his whole conversation.[46]

John Stoughton said, "His piety equaled his erudition."[47] Thomas Chalmers of Scotland commented on Owen's book *On the Nature, Power, Deceit, and Prevalence of Indwelling Sin in Believers*, "It is most important to be instructed on this subject by one who had reached such lofty attainments in holiness, and whose profound and experimental [experiential] acquaintance

---

[45] Ibid., p. 41.
[46] Ibid., p. 173.
[47] *A Religious Encyclopedia*, Vol. 2, p. 1712

with the spiritual life so well fitted him for expounding its nature and operations."[48]

Why We Need to Listen to John Owen

The reason this question of personal holiness is so urgent for us today is not only because there is a "holiness without which no one will see the Lord" (Hebrews 12:14), but also because there seems to be a shortage of political and ecclesiastical leaders today who make the quest for holiness as central as the quest for church growth or academic achievement or political success. In recent years even a President of the United States has communicated clearly that he did not think his personal morality was a significant factor in his leadership of the nation. The cavalier way that many church leaders treat sexual propriety is an echo of the same disease. John Owen would have been astonished at both the national and the ecclesiastical scene in America.

John Owen is a good counselor and model for us on this matter of holiness because he was not a hermit. We often think that some people have the monkish luxury of just staying out of the mess of public life and becoming holy people. Not so the Puritans of Owen's day. J. I. Packer said that Puritanism was "a reformed monasticism outside the cloister and away from monkish vows."[49] This is especially true of Owen.

---

[48] *Works* I:lxxxiv.
[49] Packer, *A Quest for Godliness*, p. 28.

The Great Doer

His contemporary, Richard Baxter, called Owen "the great doer."[50] He lived in the public eye. He was involved in academic administration; he was in politics up to his ears; he was entangled with the leading military officers of the country; he was embroiled in controversies over all kinds of matters from the authenticity of the Hebrew vowel points and the Epistle of Ignatius to the national laws of toleration and the nature of justification. He was looked to by thousands of congregational independent ministers as their spokesman at the national level; he was all the while pastoring people—and, we must not forget, losing a child in death every three years.

The Cost of Public Faithfulness: Criticism

We all know that a life like this is shot through with criticism that can break the spirit and make the quest for personal holiness doubly difficult. When his adversaries could not better him in argument, they resorted to character assassination. He was called "the great bell-wether of disturbance and sedition . . . a person who would have vied with Mahomet himself both for boldness and imposture . . . a viper, so swollen with venom that it must either burst or spit its poison."[51]

And even more painful and disheartening was the criticism of friends. He once got a critical letter from John Eliot, the missionary to the Indians in America, that wounded him more deeply, he said, than any of his adversaries. He wrote to Eliot:

---

[50] Toon, *God's Statesman*, p. 95.
[51] *Works*, I:lxxxix.

> What I have received from you . . . hath printed deeper, and
> left a greater impression upon my mind, than all the viru-
> lent revilings and false accusations I have met withal from
> my professed adversaries. . . . That I should now be appre-
> hended to have given a wound unto *holiness* in the
> churches, it is one of the saddest frowns in the cloudy
> brows of Divine Providence.[52]

Add to this the daily burdens of living in a pre-technological world
with no modern conveniences and passing through two major
plagues, one of which in 1665 killed seventy thousand of the
half-million people in London,[53] plus the twenty years of living
outside the protection of the law—then we know that John
Owen's holiness was not worked out in the comforts of peace
and leisure and safety. When a man like this, under these circumstances, is remembered and extolled for centuries for his personal holiness we should listen.

How Owen Pursued Private and Public Holiness

Owen's personal holiness and public fruitfulness did not just happen to him. He pursued them. There were strategies of personal
discipline and public authenticity that God used to make him
what he was. In all our life and ministry, as we care for people
and contend for the faith, we can learn much from Owen's pursuit
of holiness in private and public.

---

[52] Toon, ed., *The Correspondence of John Owen*, p. 154.
[53] Toon, *God's Statesman*, p. 131.

Owen Humbled Himself Under the Mighty Hand of God

Though he was one of the most influential and well-known men of his day, his own view of his place in God's economy was sober and humble. Two days before he died he wrote in a letter to Charles Fleetwood, "I am leaving the ship of the Church in a storm, but while the great Pilot is in it the loss of a poor under-rower will be inconsiderable."[54]

Packer says that "Owen, [though] a proud man by nature, had been brought low in and by his conversion, and thereafter he kept himself low by recurring contemplation of his inbred sinfulness."[55] Owen illustrates this:

> To keep our souls in a constant state of mourning and self-abasement is the most necessary part of our wisdom . . . and it is so far from having any inconsistency with those consolations and joys, which the gospel tenders unto us in believing, as that it is the only way to let them into the soul in a due manner.[56]

With regard to his immense learning and the tremendous insight he had into the things of God he seems to have a humbler attitude toward his achievement because he had climbed high enough to see over the first ridge of revelation into the endless mysteries of God.

> I make no pretence of searching into the bottom or depths of any part of this "great mystery of godliness, God manifest in the flesh." They are altogether unsearchable, unto

---

[54] Toon, ed., *The Correspondence of John Owen*, p. 174.
[55] Packer, *A Quest for Godliness*, p. 193.
[56] *Works*, VII:532.

the [limit] of the most enlightened minds, in this life. What
we shall farther comprehend of them in the other world,
God only knows.[57]

This humility opened Owen's soul to the greatest visions of Christ
in the Scriptures. And he believed with all his heart the truth of
2 Corinthians 3:18, that by contemplating the glory of Christ
"we may be gradually transformed into the same glory."[58] And
that is nothing other than holiness.

Owen Grew in Knowledge by Obeying What He Knew

Owen recognized that holiness is not merely the goal of all true
learning; it is also one crucial means of more true learning. This
elevated holiness even higher in his life: it was the aim of his life
and, in large measure, the means of getting there.

> The true notion of *holy evangelical truths* will not *live*, at
> least not *flourish*, where they are divided from a holy con-
> versation [=life]. As we learn all to practise, so we learn
> much by practice. . . .
>   And hereby alone can we come unto the *assurance*
> that what we know and learn is indeed the truth [cf.
> John 7:17]. . . . And hereby will they be led continually
> into farther degrees of knowledge; for the mind of man
> is capable of receiving *continual supplies* in the increase
> of light and knowledge . . . if . . . they are improved
> unto their proper end in obedience unto God. But with-
> out this the mind will be quickly stuffed with notions,

---

[57] *Works*, I:44; cf. VI:64, 68.
[58] *God's Statesman*, p. 175; *Works*, I:275.

so that no streams can descend into it from the fountain of truth.[59]

Thus Owen kept the streams of the fountain of truth open by making personal obedience the effect of all that he learned.

Owen Passionately Pursued a Personal Communion with God

It is incredible that Owen was able, under the pressures of his life, to keep writing books that were both weighty and edifying. Andrew Thomson, one of his biographers, wrote,

> It is interesting to find the ample evidence which [his work on *Mortification*] affords, that amid the din of theological controversy, the engrossing and perplexing activities of a high public station, and the chilling damps of a university, he was yet living near God, and like Jacob amid the stones of the wilderness, maintaining secret intercourse with the eternal and invisible.[60]

Packer says that the Puritans differ from evangelicals today because with them

> communion with God was a *great* thing, to evangelicals today it is a comparatively *small* thing. The Puritans were concerned about communion with God in a way that we are not. The measure of our unconcern is the little that we say about it. When Christians meet, they talk to each other about their Christian work and Christian interests,

---

[59] *Works*, IV:206, italics in original.
[60] Owen, *Works*, I:lxiv-lxv.

their Christian acquaintances, the state of the churches, and the problems of theology—but rarely of their daily experience of God.[61]

But God was seeing to it that Owen and the suffering Puritans of his day lived closer to God and sought after communion with God more earnestly than we. Writing a letter during an illness in 1674 Owen said to a friend, "Christ is our best friend, and ere long will be our only friend. I pray God with all my heart that I may be weary of everything else but converse and communion with Him."[62] God was using illness and all the other pressures of Owen's life to drive him into communion with God and not away from it.

Severest Thought for the Contemplation of Christ

But Owen was also very intentional about his communion with God. He said, "Friendship is most maintained and kept up by visits; and these, the more free and less occasioned by urgent business. . . ."[63] In other words, in the midst of all his academic and political and ecclesiastical labors he made many visits to his Friend, Jesus Christ.

And when he went, he did not just go with petitions for things or even for deliverance in his many hardships. He went to see his glorious friend and to contemplate his greatness. The last book he wrote—he was finishing it as he died—is called *Meditations*

---

[61] Packer, *A Quest for Godliness*, p. 215.
[62] Toon, *God's Statesman*, p. 153.
[63] Owen, *Works*, VII:197ff.

on the Glory of Christ. That says a great deal about the focus and outcome of Owen's life. In it he said:

> The revelation . . . of Christ . . . deserves the severest of our thoughts, the best of our meditations and our utmost diligence in them. . . . What better preparation can there be for [our future enjoyment of the glory of Christ] than in a constant previous contemplation of that glory in the revelation that is made in the Gospel.[64]

The contemplation Owen has in mind is made up of at least two things: on the one hand there is what he called his "severest thoughts" and "best meditations," or in another place "assiduous meditations," and, on the other hand, relentless prayer. The two are illustrated in his work on Hebrews.

Assiduous Meditation, Constant Prayer

One of his greatest achievements was his seven-volume commentary on Hebrews. When he finished it near the end of his life he said, "Now my work is done: it is time for me to die."[65] How did he do it? We get a glimpse from the preface:

> I must now say, that, after all my searching and reading, *prayer and assiduous meditation* have been my only resort, and by far the most useful means of light and assistance. By these have my thoughts been freed from many an entanglement.[66]

---

[64] Owen, *Works*, I:275.
[65] Toon, *God's Statesman*, p. 168.
[66] Owen, *Works* I:lxxxv. Italics added.

Whether it is for the sake of the holiness of our own soul or the ability to discern and answer the "madness" of false teachers, Owen repeatedly commended serious study of the Scriptures combined with "continual attendance on the throne of grace."

> Diligent, constant, serious reading, studying, meditating on the Scriptures, with the assistance and direction of all the rules and advantages for the right understanding of them . . . accompanied with continual attendance on the throne of grace for the presence of the Spirit of truth with us, to lead us into all truth, and to increase his anointing of us day by day, "shining into our hearts to give us the knowledge of the glory of God in the face of Jesus Christ," is . . . for our preservation against these abominations, and the enabling of us to discover their madness and answer their objections, of indispensable necessity.[67]

His aim in all he did was to grasp the mind of Christ and reflect it in his behavior. This means that the quest for holiness was always bound up with a quest for true knowledge of God. That's why prayer and study and meditation always went together.

> I suppose . . . this may be fixed on as a common principle of Christianity; namely, that constant and fervent prayer for the divine assistance of the Holy Spirit, is such an indispensable means for . . . attaining the knowledge of the mind of God in the Scripture, as that without it all others will not [avail].[68]

---

[67] Owen, *Works* XII:50.
[68] Owen, *Works*, IV:203.

Owen gives us a glimpse into the struggle that we all have in this regard lest anyone think he was above the battle. He wrote to John Eliot in New England,

> I do acknowledge unto you that I have a dry and barren spirit, and I do heartily beg your prayers that the Holy One would, notwithstanding all my sinful provocations, water me from above.[69]

In other words, the prayers of others, not just his own, were essential for his holiness.

The source of all that Owen preached and wrote was this "assiduous meditation" on Scripture and prayer. Which leads us to the fourth way that Owen achieved such holiness in his immensely busy and productive life.

Commending in Public Only What He Experienced in Private

One great hindrance to holiness in the ministry of the Word is that we are prone to preach and write without pressing into the things we say and making them real to our own souls. Over the years words begin to come easy, and we find we can speak of mysteries without standing in awe; we can speak of purity without feeling pure; we can speak of zeal without spiritual passion; we can speak of God's holiness without trembling; we can speak of sin without sorrow; we can speak of heaven without eagerness. And the result is an increasing hardening of the spiritual life.

Words came easy for Owen, but he set himself against this

---

[69] Toon, ed., *The Correspondence of John Owen*, p. 154.

terrible disease of inauthenticity and secured his growth in holiness. He began with the premise: "Our happiness consisteth not in the *knowing* the things of the gospel, but in the *doing* of them."[70] Doing, not just knowing, was the goal of all his studies.

As a means to this authentic doing he labored to experience every truth he preached. He said,

> I hold myself bound in conscience and in honor, not even to imagine that I have attained a proper knowledge of any one article of truth, much less to publish it, unless through the Holy Spirit I have had such a taste of it, in its spiritual sense, that I may be able, from the heart, to say with the psalmist, "I have believed, and therefore I have spoken."[71]

So, for example, his *Exposition of Psalm 130* (320 pages on eight verses) is the laying open not only of the Psalm but of his own heart. Andrew Thomson says,

> When Owen . . . laid open the book of God, he laid open at the same time the book of his own heart and of his own history, and produced a book which . . . is rich in golden thoughts, and instinct with the living experience of "one who spake what he knew, and testified what he had seen."[72]

The same biographer said of Owen's *On The Grace and Duty of Being Spiritually Minded* (1681) that he "first preached [it] to his own heart, and then to a private congregation; and which reveals

---

[70] Owen, *Works* XIV:311.
[71] Owen, *Works*, X:488.
[72] Owen, *Works* I:lxxxiv.

to us the almost untouched and untrodden eminences on which Owen walked in the last years of his pilgrimage."[73]

Communing with God in the Doctrine We Contend for

The conviction that controlled Owen in this was the following:

> A man preacheth that sermon only well unto others which preacheth itself in his own soul. And he that doth not feed on and thrive in the digestion of the food which he provides for others will scarce make it savory unto them; yea, he knows not but the food he hath provided may be poison, unless he have really tasted of it himself. If the word do not dwell with power *in* us, it will not pass with power *from* us.[74]

It was this conviction that sustained Owen in his immensely busy public life of controversy and conflict. Whenever he undertook to defend a truth, he sought first of all to take that truth deeply into his heart and gain a real spiritual experience of it so that there would be no artificiality in the debate and no mere posturing or gamesmanship. He was made steady in the battle because he had come to experience the truth at the personal level of the fruits of holiness and knew that God was in it. Here is the way he put it in the Preface to *The Mystery of the Gospel Vindicated* (1655):

> When the heart is cast indeed into the mould of the doctrine that the mind embraceth—when the evidence and necessity of the truth abides in us—when not the sense of the words only is in our heads, but the sense of the

[73] Ibid., p. xcix-c.
[74] Owen, *Works*, XVI:76.

thing abides in our hearts—when we have communion
with God in the doctrine we contend for—then shall we
be garrisoned by the grace of God against all the assaults
of men.[75]

That, I think, was the key to Owen's life and ministry, so
renowned for holiness—"when we have *communion* with God
in the *doctrine* we contend for—then shall we be garrisoned by the
grace of God against all the assaults of men."

Preparing to Meet Christ

The last thing Owen was doing, as the end of his life approached,
was communing with Christ in a work that was later published
as *Meditations on the Glory of Christ*. His friend William Payne
was helping him edit the work. Near the end Owen said, "O,
brother Payne, the long-wished for day is come at last, in which I
shall see the glory in another manner than I have ever done or
was capable of doing in this world."[76]

John Owen contended for the fullness of biblical faith because
he wanted generations after him to enjoy that same "long-wished
for day" when we will see the glory of Christ "in another manner"
than we have ever seen it here. He knew that our final salvation
depends on our present seeing of the glory of Christ in the gospel
(2 Corinthians 4:4). And he knew that it is the pure in heart who
see this glory (Matthew 5:8). The purifying work of the Holy
Spirit opens us to see and savor the glory of God in the face of
Christ. This spiritual sight, in turn, enables us to be more and

---

[75] Owen, *Works* XII:52.
[76] Toon, *God's Statesman*, p. 171.

more conformed to Christ (2 Corinthians 3:18). Therefore Owen saw the intimate connection between contending for the gospel and being consecrated by the gospel. He never made controversy, nor its victory, an end in itself.[77] The end was to see Jesus Christ, be satisfied with him, and be transformed into his likeness. For this great spiritual transaction there must be Spirit and truth. And that meant, in his day, consecration and controversy. Prayer and study. Faith and a fight to preserve its foundation for others.

I thank God for John Owen's unwavering passion for communion with God. I thank God that this passion motivated his fierce attack on his own unholiness, and that it proved to be the "key to Owen's own steadfastness amid all those winds of doctrine which unsettled" his century.[78] We are debtors to his mighty pen and to the passion for God's glory and his own holiness that drove it.

---

[77] "It is the direction, satisfaction, and peace of the consciences of men, and not the curiosity of notions or subtlety of deputations, which it is our duty to design." John Owen, *Works*, V:8.

[78] Andrew Thomson wrote: "This secret communion with God in the doctrines contended for was the true key to Owen's own steadfastness amid all those winds of doctrine which unsettled every thing but what was rooted in the soil." *Works* I:lxiv.

As for me, I believe that a great opportunity has been opened to Christian people by the "controversy" that is so much decried. Conventions have been broken down; men are trying to penetrate beneath pious words to the thing that these words designate; it is becoming increasingly necessary for a man to choose whether he will stand with Christ or against Him. Such a condition, I for my part believe, has been brought about by the Spirit of God; already there has been genuine spiritual advance. It has been signally manifested at the institution which I have the honor to serve [Princeton Seminary]. . . .
During the academic year, 1924-25, there has been something like an awakening. Youth has begun to think for itself; the evil of compromising associations has been discovered; Christian heroism in the face of opposition has come again to its rights; a new interest has been aroused in the historical and philosophical questions that underlie the Christian religion; true and independent convictions have been formed.
Controversy, in other words, has resulted in a striking intellectual and spiritual advance. Some of us discern in all this the work of the Spirit of God. . . .Controversy of the right sort is good; for out of such controversy, as Church history and Scripture alike teach, there comes the salvation of souls.

J. GRESHAM MACHEN, *WHAT IS FAITH?*
(1925; REPRINT: EDINBURGH:
BANNER OF TRUTH, 1991), PP. 42-43

3

CONTENDING FOR FACTS
FOR THE SAKE OF FAITH

J. Gresham Machen's Constructive Controversy with Modernism

The Tragic End in Midlife

On New Year's Eve, 1936, in a Roman Catholic hospital in Bismarck, North Dakota, J. Gresham Machen was one day away from death at the age of fifty-five. It was Christmas break at Westminster Seminary in Philadelphia where he taught New Testament. His colleagues had said he looked "deadly tired" at the end of the term. But instead of resting, he had taken the train from Philadelphia to the 20-below-zero winds of North Dakota to preach in a few Presbyterian churches at the request of pastor Samuel Allen.

Ned Stonehouse, his New Testament assistant said, "There was no one of sufficient influence to constrain him to curtail his program to any significant degree."[1] He was the acknowledged

---

[1] Ned B. Stonehouse, *J. Gresham Machen: A Biographical Memoir* (1954; reprint: Edinburgh: Banner of Truth Trust, 1987), p. 506. This volume was published seventeen years after Machen's death.

leader of the conservative movement in Presbyterianism with no one to watch over him. His heroes and mentors, Warfield and Patton, were dead. He had never married, and so had no wife to restrain him with reality. His mother and father, who gave him so much wise counsel over the years, were dead. His two brothers lived fifteen hundred miles east of where he lay dying. "He had a personality that only his good friends found appealing."[2] And so he was remarkably alone and isolated for a man of international stature.

He had pneumonia and could scarcely breathe. Pastor Allen came to pray for him that last day of 1936, and Machen told him of a vision that he had had of being in heaven. "Sam, it was glorious, it was glorious," he said. And a little later he added, "Sam, isn't the Reformed Faith grand?"

The following day—New Year's Day, 1937—he mustered the strength to send a telegram to John Murray, his friend and colleague at Westminster. It was his last recorded word: "I'm so thankful for [the] active obedience of Christ. No hope without it." He died about 7:30 P.M.

So much of the man is here in this tragic scene. The stubbornness of going his own way when friends urged him not to take this extra preaching trip. His isolation far from the mainline centers of church life and thought. His suffering for the cause he believed in. His utter allegiance to, and exaltation of, the Reformed Faith of the Westminster Confession. And his taking comfort not just from a general truth about Christ, but from a doctrinally precise understanding of the *active* obedience of

[2] George Marsden, "Understanding J. Gresham Machen," in *Understanding Fundamentalism and Evangelicalism* (Grand Rapids, MI: Eerdmans, 1991), p. 200.

Christ—which he believed was credited to his account and would make him a suitable heir of eternal life, for Christ's sake.

The Institutional Fruit of His Life

And so Machen was cut off in the midst of a great work—the establishment of Westminster Seminary and the Orthodox Presbyterian Church. He hadn't set out to found a seminary or a new church. But given who he was and what he stood for and what was happening at Princeton, where he had taught for twenty-three years, and in the Presbyterian Church in the U.S.A., it was almost inevitable.

Westminster Seminary was seven years old when Machen died. The Presbyterian Church in America (which was forced under law to change its name and became the Orthodox Presbyterian Church) was six months old, and Machen had been elected the first Moderator on June 11, 1936.

The Fateful Charge of Insubordination

The occasion for starting a new Presbyterian church over against the huge Presbyterian Church in the U.S.A. was that on March 29, 1935, Machen's Presbytery in Trenton, New Jersey found him guilty of insubordination to church authorities[3] and stripped him of his ordination. An appeal was taken to the General Assembly at Syracuse in the summer of 1936 but failed.

The reason for the charge of insubordination was that Machen had founded an independent board of foreign missions in

---

[3] See Stonehouse, *J. Gresham Machen*, p. 489 for the list of grievances.

June 1933 to protest the fact that the Presbyterian Board of
Foreign Missions endorsed a laymen's report (called *Rethinking
Missions*) that Machen said, was "from beginning to end an
attack upon the historic Christian faith."[4]

He pointed out that the board supported missionaries like
Pearl Buck in China who represented the kind of evasive, non-
committal attitude toward Christian truth that Machen thought
was destroying the church and its witness. She said, for example,
that if someone existed who could create a person like Christ
and portray him for us, "then Christ lived and lives, whether He
was once one body and one soul, or whether He is the essence of
men's highest dreams."[5]

How serious was it that Machen could not give or endorse giving to this board? The General Assembly gave answer in
Cleveland in 1934 with this astonishing sentence:

> A church member . . . that will not give to promote the
> officially authorized missionary program of the
> Presbyterian Church is in exactly the same position with
> reference to the Constitution of the Church as a church
> member . . . that would refuse to take part in the cele-
> bration of the Lord's Supper or any other prescribed ordi-
> nance of the denomination.[6]

Thus Machen was forced by his own conscience into what the
church viewed as the gravest insubordination and disobedience
to his ordination vows and removed him from the ministry. Hence
the beginning of the Orthodox Presbyterian Church.

---

[4] Ibid., p. 475.
[5] Ibid., p. 474.
[6] Ibid., p. 485.

"Princeton Seminary Is Dead"

A few years earlier Machen had left Princeton Seminary to found Westminster Seminary. This time he wasn't forced out, but chose freely to leave when the governing boards of the seminary were reorganized so that the conservative Board of Directors could be diluted by liberals[7] more in tune with President Stevensen and with the denomination as a whole.[8] Machen said,

> If the proposed . . . dissolution of the present Board of Directors is finally carried out . . . [and] the control of the Seminary passes into entirely different hands—then Princeton Theological Seminary as it has been so long and so honorably known, will be dead, and we shall have at Princeton a new institution of radically different type.[9]

Well, Princeton Seminary did die, in Machen's eyes, and out of the ashes he meant to preserve the tradition of Charles Hodge and Benjamin Warfield. So when he gave the inaugural address of Westminster Seminary on September 25, 1929, to the first class of fifty students and guests, he said,

> No, my friends, though Princeton Seminary is dead, the noble tradition of Princeton Seminary is alive. Westminster Seminary will endeavor by God's grace to continue that tradition unimpaired.[10]

---

[7] To prove the doctrinal drift of the action to reorganize the seminary, two signers of the liberal "Auburn Affirmation" were appointed to the new board. Ibid., p. 441.
[8] Ibid., p. 422.
[9] Ibid., p. 427.
[10] Ibid., p. 458.

Machen's most enduring response to modernism was the founding of these two institutions: Westminster Seminary (which today
is a major influence in American evangelicalism) and the
Orthodox Presbyterian Church (which now, over six decades later,
bears a witness disproportionate to its small size[11]).

Where Did This Warrior Come from?

Who was J. Gresham Machen? Where did he come from? What
shaped and drove him? More important than the mere fact of
founding institutions is the question of the worldview that carried him through that achievement. And what was this thing
called "Modernism" that engaged his amazingly energetic opposition? And what can we learn from his response today?

John Gresham Machen was born in Baltimore, Maryland,
on July 28, 1881, sixteen years after the Civil War. His mother was
from Macon, Georgia, and was educated and cultured enough
that she published a book in 1903 entitled *The Bible in Browning*.
His father was a very successful lawyer from Baltimore. The family hobnobbed with the cultural elite in Baltimore, had a vaca-
tion home in Seal Harbor, Maine, and traveled often. Machen
sailed to Europe and back some six times. In a word Machen
was a well-to-do southern aristocrat.

He went to the private University School for Boys where
classics (especially Latin) were stressed from the time he was
eleven. The family were devoted members of Franklin St.

---

[11] For a testimony to the life and witness of the Orthodox Presbyterian Church see Charles
Dennison and Richard Gamble, eds., *Pressing Toward the Mark: Essays Commemorating
Fifty Years of the Orthodox Presbyterian Church* (Philadelphia: The Committee for the
Historian of the Orthodox Presbyterian Church, 1986).

Presbyterian Church, which was a part of the Southern Presbyterian Church.

A Son of Southern Culture for Better or Worse

This cultural atmosphere shaped Machen's views and sentiments in various ways. For example, he shared the southern paternalistic attitudes toward African-Americans. In an essay for his first year at Johns Hopkins University when he was seventeen he wrote of his home: "The servants are the real, old-fashioned kind-hearted Southern darkies."[12] His view of the southern cause in the Civil War, still fresh in everyone's mind, was the same as his favorite professor's at Johns Hopkins:

> That the cause we fought for and our brothers died for was the cause of civil liberty and not the cause of human slavery . . . It was a point of grammatical concord that was at the bottom of the Civil War—"United States are," said one, "United States is," said another.[13]

Being a southerner—or part of any other culture for that matter—has its advantages and disadvantages in creating our blind spots and opening our eyes. George Marsden suggests that some of Machen's insight into the cultural movements of his day may be owing to his Southern roots: "Machen as a Southerner may have something to offer us. As a Southerner Machen was an outsider to the mainline Protestant establishment and hence may

---

[12] Stonehouse, *J. Gresham Machen*, p. 46.

[13] Ibid., p. 50. The professor was B. L. Gildersleeve whose specialty was the history of American classical scholarship.

again have been alert to important trends that others were not seeing."[14]

Machen Was Wealthy

When he was twenty-one he inherited $50,000 from his maternal grandfather. To put that in perspective, his first *annual* salary at Princeton was $2,000. So he inherited twenty-five times an annual salary when he was twenty-one, and when he was thirty-five he inherited a similar amount when his father died. When he died, his assets totaled $250,000 dollars.[15] This explains why we can read time after time of Machen's funding ministry and publishing efforts with his own money.

As with most of us, therefore, the level at which Machen engaged the culture of his day was being powerfully shaped by the level of his upbringing and education. He went to Johns Hopkins University and majored in Classics and then, with the urging of his pastor, went on to Princeton Seminary, even though he was not at all sure he would enter the ministry. And after seminary he spent a year in Germany studying New Testament with well-known German scholars.

The Threats and Blessings of the German University

Here Machen met Modernism face to face and was shaken profoundly in his faith. Almost overpowering was the influence of Wilhelm Herrmann, the systematic theologian at Marburg, who

---

[14] Marsden, "Understanding J. Gresham Machen," p. 199.
[15] Stonehouse, *J. Gresham Machen*, p. 393.

represented the best of what Machen would later oppose with all his might. He was not casting stones over a wall when he criticized Modernism. Machen had been over the wall and was almost lured into the camp.

In 1905 he wrote home:

> The first time that I heard Herrmann may almost be described as an epoch in my life. Such an overpowering personality I think I almost never before encountered— overpowering in the sincerity of religious devotion. . . .
>
> My chief feeling with reference to him is already one of the deepest reverence. . . . I have been thrown all into confusion by what he says—so much deeper is his devotion to Christ than anything I have known in myself during the past few years. . . . Herrmann affirms very little of that which I have been accustomed to regard as essential to Christianity; yet there is no doubt in my mind but that he is a Christian, and a Christian of a peculiarly earnest type. He is a Christian not because he follows Christ as a moral teacher; but because his trust in Christ is (practically, if anything even more truly than theoretically) unbounded. . . .
>
> Herrmann represents the dominant Ritschlian school . . . . Herrmann has shown me something of the *religious* power which lies back of this great movement, which is now making a fight even for the control of the Northern Presbyterian Church in America. In New England those who do not believe in the bodily Resurrection of Jesus are, generally speaking, religiously dead; in Germany, Herrmann has taught me that is by no means the case. He believes that Jesus is the one thing in all the world that inspires *absolute* confidence, and an *absolute*, joyful subjection; that through Jesus we come into communion with the living God and are made free from the world. It is the faith that is a real experience, a real revelation of God

that saves us, not the faith that consists in accepting as true a lot of dogmas on the basis merely of what others have said. . . . *Das Verkehr des Christen mit Gott* is one of the greatest religious books I ever read. Perhaps Herrmann does not give the whole truth—I certainly hope he does not—at any rate he has gotten hold of something that has been sadly neglected in the church and in the orthodox theology. Perhaps he is something like the devout mystics of the middle ages—they were one-sided enough, but they raised a mighty protest against the coldness and deadness of the church and were forerunners of the Reformation.[16]

The Lasting Impact of His German Experience

What Machen seemed to find in Herrmann was what he had apparently not found either in his home or at Princeton, namely, passion and joy and exuberant trust in Christ. At Princeton he had found solid learning and civil, formal, careful, aristocratic presentations of a fairly cool Christianity. He eventually came to see that the truth of the Princeton theology was a firmer ground for life and joy. But at this stage the spirit in which it came, compared to Herrmann's spirit, almost cost evangelicalism one of its greatest defenders. There is a great lesson here for teachers and preachers: to hold young minds there should be both intellectual credibility *and* joyful, passionate zeal for Christ.

This experience in Germany made a lasting impact on the way Machen carried on controversy. He said again and again that he had respect and sympathy for the modernist who could honestly no longer believe in the bodily resurrection or the virgin birth or

---

[16] Ibid., pp. 106-108. This quote is a composite of excerpts from letters that year to his parents and brother.

the second coming, but it was the rejection of these things without openly admitting one's unbelief that angered Machen.

For example, he said once that his problem with certain teachers at Union Seminary was their duplicity:

> There is my real quarrel with them. As for their difficulties with the Christian faith, I have profound sympathy for them, but not with their contemptuous treatment of the conscientious men who believe that a creed solemnly subscribed to is more than a scrap of paper.[17]

He wanted to deal with people in a straightforward manner, and take his opponents' arguments seriously if they would only be honest and open with their constituents and readers.

The Fruit of Doubt

His struggle with doubt gave him patience and empathy with others in the same situation. Twenty years later he wrote,

> Some of us have been through such struggle ourselves; some of us have known the blankness of doubt, the deadly discouragement, the perplexity of indecision, the vacillation between "faith diversified by doubt," and "doubt diversified by faith."[18]

Machen came through this time without losing his evangelical faith and was called to Princeton to teach New Testament, which he did from 1906 until he left to form Westminster in

---

[17] Ibid., pp. 221-222.
[18] Ibid., p. 432.

1929. During that time he became a pillar of conservative, reformed orthodoxy and a strong apologist for biblical Christianity and an internationally acclaimed New Testament scholar with his book, *The Origin of Paul's Religion*, published in 1921 (still used as a text at Fuller Seminary when I went there in 1968), and then his most famous book, *The Virgin Birth of Christ* in 1930.

Was Machen a Fundamentalist?

Machen's years at Princeton were the two decades that are known for the ongoing modernist-fundamentalist controversy. We will see Machen's distinctive response to Modernism if we contrast it with what was known most widely as Fundamentalism. In the process of defining his response, the meaning of Modernism will become clear.

He was seen as an ally by the fundamentalists; and his ecclesiastical opponents liked to make him "guilty" by association with them. But he did not accept the term for himself. In one sense fundamentalists were simply those who "[singled] out certain great facts and doctrines [i.e., fundamentals] that had come under particular attack, [and] were concerned to emphasize their truth and to defend them."[19] But there was more attached to the term than that. And Machen didn't like it. He said:

> Do you suppose that I do regret my being called by a term that I greatly dislike, a "Fundamentalist"? Most certainly I do. But in the presence of a great common foe, I have

---

[19] Ibid., p. 336.

little time to be attacking my brethren who stand with me in defense of the Word of God.[20]

What he didn't like was

- the absence of historical perspective;

- the lack of appreciation of scholarship;

- the substitution of brief, skeletal creeds for the historic confessions;

- the lack of concern with precise formulation of Christian doctrine;

- the pietistic, perfectionist tendencies (i.e., hang-ups with smoking,[21] etc.);

- one-sided otherworldliness (i.e., a lack of effort to transform culture); and

- a penchant for futuristic chiliasm (or: premillennialism).

Machen was on the other side on all these issues. And so "he never spoke of himself as a Fundamentalist."[22]

Calvinism Is Christianity in Full Flower

But none of those issues goes to the heart of why he did not see himself as a fundamentalist. The issue is deeper and broader and gets at the root of how he fought Modernism. The deepest difference goes back to Machen's profound indebtedness to Benjamin

---

[20] Ibid., p. 337.

[21] In 1905 as his seminary days were coming to an end he wrote, "The fellows are in my room now on the last Sunday night, smoking the cigars and eating the oranges which it has been the greatest delight I ever had to provide whenever possible. My idea of delight is a Princeton room full of fellows smoking. When I think what a wonderful aid tobacco is to friendship and Christian patience, I have sometimes regretted that I never began to smoke". Ibid., p. 85.

[22] Ibid., p. 337. See "Does Fundamentalism Obstruct Social Progress?" and "What Fundamentalism Stands For Now," in *J. Gresham Machen: Selected Shorter Writings*, ed. D. G. Hart (Phillipsburg, NJ: P&R, 2004), pp. 109-122.

Warfield, who died February 16, 1921. Machen wrote to his mother, "With all his glaring faults he was the greatest man I have known."[23]

In 1909 at the 400th anniversary of John Calvin's birth Warfield gave an address that stirred Machen to the depths. Warfield made a plea that the Reformed Faith—Calvinism—is not a species of Christian theism alongside others but *is* Christianity come to full flower.

> Calvinism is not a specific variety of theistic thought, religious experience, [or] evangelical faith; but just the perfect expression of these things. The difference between it and other forms of Theism, religion, [and] evangelicalism is a difference not of kind but of degree.... It does not take its position then by the side of other types of things; it takes its place over them, as what they ought to be.[24]

So he says Lutheranism is "its sister type of Protestantism" and Arminianism is "its own rebellious daughter."[25] Calvinism's grasp of the supremacy of God in all of life enabled Machen to see that other forms of evangelicalism were all stages of grasping God that are yet in process of coming to a full and pure appreciation of his total God-centeredness.

What this came to mean for Machen was that his mission in defense of supernaturalistic Calvinism was nothing more or less than the defense of the Christian faith in its purest form. So his

---

[23] Stonehouse, *J. Gresham Machen*, p. 310. George Marsden quotes a letter from Machen on October 5, 1913 in which he said that Warfield was "himself, despite some very good qualities, a very heartless, selfish, domineering sort of man." "Understanding J. Gresham Machen," p. 187. My interpretation of this is that there were things about Warfield that irritated Machen, but Warfield's strengths were such that they made these things pale in comparison.

[24] B. B. Warfield, "Calvinism," in *The Works of Benjamin B. Warfield*, Vol. 9 (reprint: Grand Rapids, MI: Baker, 2000), pp. 355-356.

[25] Ibid., p. 177.

biggest problem with the term *fundamentalist* was that "it seems to suggest that we are adherents of some strange new sect, whereas in point of fact we are conscious simply of maintaining the historic Christian faith and of moving in the great central current of Christian life."[26]

He was invited to the presidency of Bryan Memorial University in 1927—a move that would have aligned him with Fundamentalism outside the Reformed tradition. He answered:

> Thoroughly consistent Christianity, to my mind, is found only in the Reformed or Calvinist Faith; and consistent Christianity, I think, is the Christianity easiest to defend. Hence I never call myself a "Fundamentalist." . . . What I prefer to call myself is not a "Fundamentalist" but a "Calvinist"—that is, an adherent of the Reformed Faith. As such I regard myself as standing in the great central current of the Church's life—the current that flows down from the Word of God through Augustine and Calvin, and which has found noteworthy expression in America in the great tradition represented by Charles Hodge and Benjamin Breckinridge Warfield and the other representatives of the "Princeton School."[27]

Liberalism (Modernism) Is Another Religion

So Machen moved in a different world from most fundamentalists. And when he took on Modernism he took it on as a challenge to the whole of Reformed Christianity. His most important book in the debate was *Christianity and Liberalism*, published in 1923.

---

[26] Ibid., p. 337.
[27] Ibid., p. 428.

The title almost says it all: Liberalism is not vying with Fundamentalism as a species of Christianity. The book is not entitled *Fundamentalism and Liberalism*. Instead Liberalism is vying with *Christianity* as a separate religion. He wrote the blurb for the book:

> Liberalism on the one hand and the religion of the historic church on the other are not two varieties of the same religion, but two distinct religions proceeding from altogether separate roots.[28]

Stonehouse tells us that Machen's only regret is that he had not used the term *Modernism* rather than *Liberalism* in the book, since the word *Liberalism* seemed to give too much credit to the phenomenon.[29] In Machen's vocabulary, these words refer to the same thing.

Now what was that?

Here again Machen did not move quickly with the fundamentalists to show that the modernists were people who denied certain fundamental Christian doctrines. That was true. But his analysis was wider and deeper. He approached the phenomenon of Modernism first through an analysis of modern culture and the spirit of the age. He tried to think through the relationship between Modernism and modernity.[30] He wanted to understand it from the inside as it were, on its own terms.

---

[28] Ibid., p. 342.
[29] Ibid., p. 343.
[30] Notice the difference in these two terms. *Modernism* is the technical word referring to the theological response to modernity, while *modernity* refers to what Machen calls "modern culture" with its technology, science, communications, transportation, inventions, pace, and dozens of other modern phenomena.

The Roots of Modernism in Modernity

Machen admits from the outset that "modern culture is a tremendous force."[31]

> Modern inventions and the industrialism that has been
> built upon them have given us in many respects a new
> world to live in . . . [and these material conditions] have
> been produced by mighty changes in the human mind. . . .
> The industrial world of today has been produced not by
> blind forces of nature but by the conscious activity of the
> human spirit; it has been produced by the achievements
> of science.[32]

The problem of modernity is that it has bred forces that are hostile to biblical faith and yet produced a world that believers readily embrace. Machen is exactly right to skewer us in this dilemma when he says,

> We cannot without inconsistency employ the printing-
> press, the railroad, the telegraph [we in the 21st century
> would say computers, jets, and cell phones] in the propa-
> gation of our gospel, and at the same time denounce as evil
> those activities of the human mind that produced these
> things.[33]

---

[31] J. Gresham Machen, "Christianity and Culture," in *What Is Christianity and Other Addresses*, ed. Ned Stonehouse (Grand Rapids, MI: Eerdmans, 1951), p. 166.

[32] J. Gresham Machen, *Christianity and Liberalism* (1923; reprint: Grand Rapids, MI: Eerdmans, 1992), p. 3.

[33] Machen, "Christianity and Culture," p. 159.

The Impulses of Modernity

So he calls for a critical assessment of modernity.[34] The negative impulses he sees that all lead to Modernism are 1) a suspicion of the past that is natural in view of the stunning advances of recent decades; it does seem as if the past is of relatively little value; 2) skepticism about truth and a replacement of the category of true with the category of useful (pragmatism, utilitarianism); the question of what works seems to be more scientifically productive; 3) the denial that the supernatural, if there is any such thing, can break into the world.

Machen credits Modernism—the theological response to this challenge of modernity—with trying to come to terms with the real problem of the age. "What is the relation between Christianity and modern culture; may Christianity be maintained in a scientific age? It is this problem which modern liberalism attempts to solve."[35]

In trying to solve the problem, Liberalism, that is, Modernism, has joined modernity in minimizing the significance of the past in favor of newer impulses, has accepted the utilitarian view of truth, and has surrendered supernaturalism. All three compromises with the spirit of modernity work together to produce the modernist spirit in religion.

---

[34] "Modern culture is a mighty force; it is either helpful to the gospel or else it is a deadly enemy of the gospel. For making it helpful neither wholesale denunciation nor wholesale acceptance is in place; careful discrimination is required, and such discrimination requires intellectual effort. Here lies a supreme duty of the modern Church." J. Gresham Machen, *The New Testament: An Introduction to Its Literature and History* (Edinburgh: Banner of Truth, 1976), pp. 377-378.

[35] Machen, *Christianity and Liberalism*, p. 6.

Modernism Is Not Ideas but an Atmosphere of Accommodation

And it is a spirit more than a set of doctrines or denials. This is why Machen never tired of pointing out the dangers of what he called "indifferentism" and "latitudinarianism"[36] as well as the outright denials of the resurrection or the virgin birth or the inspiration of Scripture. The spirit of Modernism is not a set of ideas but an atmosphere that shifts with what is useful from time to time.

One of their own number, John A. MacCallum, an outspoken modernist minister in Philadelphia, said in a newspaper article in 1923,

> [The liberals] have accepted the enlarged view of the universe which has been established by modern astronomy, geology and biology. Instead of blindly denying scientific facts as the obscurantists have always done, they have adjusted themselves to them, and in so doing have increased their faith and urbanity and consequently extended their influence, particularly with the educated classes. . . . Liberalism is an atmosphere rather than a series of formulas.[37]

When the preference for what is new combines with a naturalistic bias and a skepticism about finding abiding truth, the stage is set for the worst abuses of religious language and the worst manipulations of historic confessions. In essence what the modernists do is not throw out Christianity but reinterpret the creeds

---

[36] For example, he says that in German universities you find "those forces which underlie all the doctrinal indifferentism in Great Britain and in this country which really presents the serious danger of the life of our Church." Stonehouse, *J. Gresham Machen*, p. 241.

[37] Stonehouse, *J. Gresham Machen*, p. 347.

and give old words new meanings. That is, they make them into symbols for ever-changing meanings.

Thus the virgin birth is one theory of the incarnation, the bodily resurrection is one theory of the resurrection, and so on. The old "facts" don't correspond to anything permanent. They symbolize general principles of religion. And those symbols are arrived at by what is useful or helpful, not by what is true. If they are useful for one generation, good; and if not for another, then they may be exchanged.

Denying Truth by Affirming It Only as Useful

This meant that in the Presbyterian Church of Machen's day there were hundreds who would not deny the Confession of Faith but by virtue of this modernistic spirit had given it up even though they'd signed it. One of the most jolting and penetrating statements of Machen on this issue is found in his book *What Is Faith?*:

> It makes very little difference how much or how little of the creeds of the Church the Modernist preacher affirms, or how much or how little of the Biblical teaching from which the creeds are derived. He might affirm every jot and tittle of the Westminster Confession, for example, and yet be separated by a great gulf from the Reformed Faith. It is not that part is denied and the rest affirmed; but all is denied, because all is affirmed merely as useful or symbolic and not as true.[38]

---

[38] Machen, *What Is Faith?* (Edinburgh: Banner of Truth, 1991, orig. 1925), p. 34.

Modernistic Hostility to Definitions

This utilitarian view of history and language leads to evasive, vague language that enables the modernist to mislead people into thinking he is still orthodox.

> This temper of mind is hostile to precise definitions. Indeed nothing makes a man more unpopular in the controversies of the present day than an insistence upon definition of terms. . . . Men discourse very eloquently today upon such subjects as God, religion, Christianity, atonement, redemption, faith; but are greatly incensed when they are asked to tell in simple language what they mean by these terms.[39]

Machen's critique of the spirit of Modernism that flows from its marriage to modernity comes from two sides. First, internally— does this modern culture really commend itself? Second, externally—does the history of Christ and the apostles really allow for such a modernistic Christianity? Or is it an alien religion?

Is Modernity as Wonderful as We Think?

Machen asks: granted, we are better off in material things because of modernity, but are we better off in the realm of the spirit and the distinctly human aspects of life?

> The improvement appears in the physical conditions of life, but in the spiritual realm there is a corresponding loss. The loss is clearest, perhaps, in the realm of art. Despite the mighty revolution which has been produced in the external condition of life, no great poet is now liv-

---

[39] Ibid., pp. 13-14.

ing to celebrate the change; humanity has suddenly
become dumb. Gone, too, are the great painters and the
great musicians and the great sculptors. The art that still
subsists is largely imitative, and where it is not imitative it
is usually bizarre.[40]

He argues that a "drab utilitarianism" destroys the higher aspi-
rations of the soul and results in an unparalleled impoverishment
of human life.[41] When you take away any objective norm of truth,
you take away the only means of measuring movement from lesser
to greater or worse to better. One doctrine is as good as any con-
tradictory doctrine "provided it suits a particular generation or a
particular group of persons." All that's left without truth are the
"meaningless changes of a kaleidoscope."[42] Without a sense of
progress in view of an objective truth, life becomes less and less,
not more and more.

In view of these and other observations about the effects of
modernity and Modernism, Machen asks modern man if he can
be so sure that the past and the truth and the supernatural are
really as cheap and expendable as he thought.

In view of the lamentable defects of modern life, a type of
religion certainly should not be commended simply
because it is modern or condemned simply because it is
old. On the contrary, the condition of mankind is such that
one may well ask what it is that made the men of past
generations so great and the men of the present generations
so small.[43]

---

[40] Machen, *Christianity and Liberalism*, p. 10.
[41] Ibid., pp. 11-12.
[42] Machen, *What Is Faith?*, p. 32.
[43] Machen, *Christianity and Liberalism*, p. 15.

Thus Machen seeks to understand and critique modernity and Modernism from the inside—and this set him off by and large from the fundamentalists of his day.

Facts Matter

Then from the outside Machen wields his powers as a historian and a student of the New Testament. He argues on historical grounds that from the beginning the church was a witnessing church (Acts 1:8) and a church devoted to the apostles' teaching. In other words, her life was built on events without which there would be no Christianity. These events demand faithful witnesses who tell the objective truth about the events since they are essential. And the life of the church was built on the apostles' teaching (Acts 2:42), the authoritative interpretation of the events.

He argues powerfully in the chapter on "Doctrine" in *Christianity and Liberalism* that Paul made much of the truth of his message and the need to get it exactly right, even if the messenger was not exactly right. For example, in Philippians he was tolerant of those who with bad motives preached in order to make his imprisonment worse—because they were saying the objective truth about Christ.

In Galatians, however, he was not tolerant but pronounced a curse on his opponents—because they were getting the message objectively wrong. They were telling Gentiles that works of the flesh would complete God's justifying action in their lives that had begun by faith and the Spirit. It may seem like a triviality since both the Judaizers and Paul would have agreed on dozens of precious things including the necessity of faith for salvation. But it was not trivial. And with this kind of historical observation and argument from the New Testament Machen shows that truth and objectivity and doctrine are not optional in grasping and spreading Christianity.

> As over against . . . [the pragmatist, modernist] attitude, we believers in historic Christianity maintain the objectivity of truth. . . . Theology, we hold, is not an attempt to express in merely symbolic terms an inner experience which must be expressed in different terms in subsequent generations; but it is a setting forth of those facts upon which experience is based.[44]

Therefore his response to Modernism stands: it is not a different kind of Christianity. It is not Christianity at all. "The chief modern rival of Christianity is 'liberalism' . . . at every point the two movements are in direct opposition."[45] The foundational truths have been surrendered; or worse, the concept of truth has been surrendered to pragmatism, so that even affirmations are denials, because they are affirmed as useful but not as true.

What Machen Saw Is Still With Us . . . So Is God

I don't think the structure of the Modernism of Machen's day is too different from the postmodernism of our day. In some churches the triumph of Modernism is complete. It is still a menace at the door of all our churches and schools and agencies. One of our great protections will be the awareness of stories like Machen's—the enemy he faced, the battle he fought, the weapons

---

[44] Machen, *What Is Faith?*, p. 32.
[45] Machen, *Christianity and Liberalism*, p. 53.

he used (and failed to use), the losses he sustained, the price he paid, and the triumphs he wrought. If we do not know history, we will be weak and poor in our efforts to be faithful in our day.

Our hope for the church and for the spread of the true gospel lies not ultimately in our strategies but in God. And there is every hope that he will triumph.

> That Church is still alive; an unbroken spiritual descent connects us with those whom Jesus commissioned. Times have changed in many respects, new problems must be faced and new difficulties overcome, but the same message must still be proclaimed to a lost world. Today we have need of all our faith; unbelief and error have perplexed us sore; strife and hatred have set the world aflame. There is only one hope, but that hope is sure. God has never deserted his church; his promise never fails.[46]

Lessons for Our Day

When we step back now and look at Machen's life and work, what can we learn for our day?

1. Machen's life and thought issues a call for all of us to be honest, open, clear, straightforward, and guileless in our use of language.

He challenges us, as does the apostle Paul (2 Corinthians 2:17; 4:2; Ephesians 4:25; 1 Thessalonians 2:3-4), to say what we mean and mean what we say, and to repudiate duplicity, trickery, sham, verbal manipulating, sidestepping, and evasion.

Machen alerts us to the dangers of the utilitarian uses of moral

---

[46] Stonehouse, *J. Gresham Machen*, p. 386.

and religious language. They are still around in our day. For example, Roy Beck quoted Gregory King, spokesman for the Human Rights Campaign Fund, the nation's largest homosexual advocacy group, who told the *Washington Times*, "I personally think that most lesbian and gay Americans support traditional family and American values," which he defined as "tolerance, concern, support, and a sense of community."[47]

This is an example of how words with moral connotations have been co-opted by special interest groups to gain the moral high ground without moral content. They sound like values, but they are empty. "Tolerance" for what? All things? Which things? The standards are not defined. "Concern" for what? Expressed in what way? Redemptive opposition or sympathetic endorsement? The standard is not defined. "Support" for what? For the behavior that is destructive and wrong? Or for the person who admits the behavior is wrong and is struggling valiantly to overcome it? The object is not defined. "Community" with what standards of unification? Common endorsements of behavior? Common vision of what is right and wrong? Common indifference to what is right and wrong? Again the standards are not defined.

Yet the opposite of each of these four "family values" (intolerant, unconcerned, oppressive, self-centered) all carry such negative connotations that it is difficult in sound bites to show why the four "values" asserted by the homosexual community are inadequate and even may be wrong as they use them.

All you have is words driven by a utilitarian view of language where honesty and truth are not paramount. Machen shows us

---

[47] *Christianity Today* 36 (November 9, 1992), p. 21.

that this is not new and that it is destructive to the church and the cause of Christ.

2. Machen alerts us to the doctrinal "indifferentism" of our day and to the fact that we almost take it for granted that utilitarian thinking is the only hope for success and that preaching or teaching doctrine is a prescription for failure.

This skepticism about the value of doctrine is owing to bad preaching that is not passionate and clear and interesting and suspenseful and authentic about the glories of God and his way of salvation, and how it all connects with real life. "The dogma is the drama,"[48] as Dorothy Sayers said, and the reason we don't show this to people in our preaching and teaching and writing is that we have not seen and felt the greatness of the glory of God and all his teachings. Preaching doctrine should not be confusing or boring. Machen says:

> That error, unquestionably, should be avoided. But it should be avoided not by the abandonment of doctrinal preaching, but by our making doctrinal preaching real *preaching*. The preacher should present to his congregation the doctrine that the Holy Scripture contains; but he should fire the presentation of that doctrine with the devotion of the heart, and he should show how it can be made fruitful for Christian life.[49]

---

[48] "Official Christianity, of late years, has been having what is known as 'a bad press.' We are constantly assured that the churches are empty because preachers insist too much upon doctrine—dull dogma as people call it. The fact is the precise opposite. It is the neglect of dogma that makes for dullness. The Christian faith is the most exciting drama that ever staggered the imagination of man—and the dogma is the drama." Dorothy L. Sayers, "The Greatest Story Ever Staged," in *Creed or Chaos? Why Christians Must Choose Either Dogma or Disaster (Or, Why It Really Does Matter What You Believe)*. Available online at http://www.modernreformation.org/ds94story.htm (accessed 8-31-05).

[49] Machen, "Christian Scholarship and the Building Up of the Church," in *What Is Christianity?*, p. 139.

3. Machen's life teaches us the importance of founding and maintaining institutions in the preservation and spreading of the true gospel.

Visions of truth and worldview like Machen's are preserved not just in the minds of a few disciples but in charters and covenants and enclaves and books and journals and durable organizations and long-term official commitments. Mark Noll observes, "The genius of Old Princeton had been its embodiment of confessional Calvinism in great institutions: the school itself, the *Princeton Review*, Hodge's *Systematic Theology*, and the Old School party among the northern Presbyterians."[50]

Founding and maintaining institutions are, of course, not the only way of spreading the truth of Christ in the world. And in the name of preserving the truth they often come to stand in the way of spreading the truth. Nevertheless they are not necessarily bad and are probably a good tension with the more charismatic, spontaneous focus on individualism in ministry.

I personally give God thanks with all my heart for the institutions of the family that I grew up in, and for Wheaton College, and for Fuller Seminary, and for the church that I now serve. By God's grace these institutions preserved and embodied for me the forces of truth and righteousness in such a way that I have been deeply shaped by them. I think if each person gives serious thought to how he came to have the convictions and values and dreams that he has, he will see that virtually all of us owe much of what we are to institutions, without denying or minimizing that it has been individual teachers, friends, and authors in and around

---

[50] Mark Noll, "The Spirit of Old Princeton and the OPC," in *Pressing Toward the Mark*, p. 245.

those institutions who have been the immediate mediators of truths and goodness and beauty.

4. Machen's experience calls us to have patience with young strugglers who are having doubts about Christianity.

Machen was saved for the kingdom and the church by faculty and parents who gave him room to work it all through. Machen says that he finally found victory and tranquillity of spirit "because of the profound and constant sympathy of others."[51]

This is illustrated especially from his mother and father who responded with love and patience to his fears that he could not enter the ministry because of his doubts. His mother wrote on January 21, 1906 while Machen was in Germany,

> But one thing I can assure you of—that *nothing* that you could do could keep me from loving you—*nothing*. It is easy enough to grieve me. Perhaps I worry too much. But my love for my boy is absolutely indestructible. Rely on that whatever comes. And I have faith in you too and believe that the strength will come to you for your work whatever it may be, and that the way will be opened.[52]

His father wrote on January 26, 1906, "None of the years of study you have had can ever be properly considered as 'wasted' no matter what field of work you may ultimately enter upon. . . . The pecuniary question you need not bother about. I can assure you on that point."[53]

Machen credits the power of his parents in his life in a letter to his father dated February 4, 1906:

---

[51] Ibid., p. 129.
[52] Ibid., p. 113.
[53] Ibid., p. 114.

Without what I got from you and Mother I should long
since have given up all thoughts of religion or of a moral
life. . . . The only thing that enables me to get any benefit
out of my opportunities here is the continual presence with
me in spirit of you and Mother and the Christian teaching which you have given me.[54]

Not only his parents but also his colleagues at Princeton in the first
several years steadied his hand and preserved his orthodox faith.
He gives amazing tribute to his closest colleague, William
Armstrong, in his installation address as Assistant Professor of
New Testament on May 3, 1915: "The assistance that he has given
me in the establishment of my Christian faith has been simply
incalculable."[55]

On July 14, 1906, Armstrong wrote to Machen with an offer
to teach that was flexible enough to allow him to begin at
Princeton on a trial basis even with some of his doubts unsettled.

You do not have to be licensed, or ordained or even come
under the care of a presbytery. You can start upon the
work just as you are. And in regard to your theological
opinions you do not have to make any pledge. You are
not expected to have reached final conclusion on all matters in this field. Only in your teaching will you be expected
to stand on the broad principles of Reformed Theology
and in particular on the authority of the Scriptures in religious matters—not that your teaching should be different
from your personal convictions—but simply that in matters not finally settled you would await decision before
departing from the position occupied by the Seminary. The

---

[54] Ibid., pp. 116-117.
[55] Ibid., p. 209.

whole matter reduces itself in simple good faith. Should you find after trying it that you could not teach in the Seminary because you had reached conclusions in your study which made it impossible for you to uphold its position you would simply say so.[56]

Machen would not have been allowed to stay at Princeton if he had come out on the wrong side or stayed indefinitely on the fence. The compromise of an institution's fidelity and the misuse of academic freedom happens when doctrinal and ethical doubts are kept secret, or, worse, when lurking denials are put forward as affirmations. Honest, humble struggles can be sustained for some season. But the duplicity that hides secret denials will destroy an institution and a soul.

5. Machen's interaction with modernism shows the value of a God-centered vision of all reality—a worldview, a theology, that is driven by the supremacy of God in all of life.

A God-centered worldview gives balance and stability in dealing with error. It enables us to see how an error relates to the larger issues of life and thought. Machen was set off from the fundamentalists by this consistently God-centered view of all things. His critique of Modernism went deeper and farther because his vision of God caused him to see the problem in a deeper and broader context. The sovereignty of God and his supremacy over all of life causes one to see everything in relation to more things because they all relate to God and God relates to all things.

6. Machen's engagement in the debates of his day points us to the value and necessity of controversy.

---

[56] Stonehouse, *J. Gresham Machen*, p. 133.

In a lecture delivered in London on June 17, 1932, Machen
defended engagement in controversy:

> Men tell us that our preaching should be positive and not
> negative, that we can preach the truth without attacking
> error. But if we follow that advice we shall have to close
> our Bible and desert its teachings. The New Testament is
> a polemic book almost from beginning to end.
>
> Some years ago I was in a company of teachers of the
> Bible in the colleges and other educational institutions of
> America. One of the most eminent theological professors
> in the country made an address. In it he admitted that there
> are unfortunate controversies about doctrine in the
> Epistles of Paul; but, said he in effect, the real essence of
> Paul's teaching is found in the hymn to Christian love in
> the thirteenth chapter of I Corinthians; and we can avoid
> controversy today, if we will only devote the chief attention
> to that inspiring hymn.
>
> In reply, I am bound to say that the example was sin-
> gularly ill-chosen. That hymn to Christian love is in the
> midst of a great polemic passage; it would never have been
> written if Paul had been opposed to controversy with
> error in the Church. It was because his soul was stirred
> within him by a wrong use of the spiritual gifts that he
> was able to write that glorious hymn. So it is always in the
> Church. Every really great Christian utterance, it may
> almost be said, is born in controversy. It is when men have
> felt compelled to take a stand against error that they have
> risen to the really great heights in the celebration of
> truth.[57]

---

[57] Machen, "Christian Scholarship and the Defense of the New Testament," in *What Is
Christianity?*, pp. 132-133. See on this same point *What Is Faith?*, pp. 41-42; *Christianity and
Liberalism*, p. 17.

7. We learn from Machen the inevitability and pain of criticism, even from our brothers.

His colleague, Charles Erdman, publicly accused Machen of "unkindness, suspicion, bitterness and intolerance."[58] When he voted against a church resolution in favor of national Prohibition and the Eighteenth Amendment, he was criticized as a secret drunkard and promoter of vice.[59] Since he was single, he was criticized as being naive and unaware of the responsibilities of the family.[60]

There is in all of us the desire to be liked by others. If it is strong enough we may go to unwise lengths to avoid criticism. We may even think that we can be kind enough to everyone to avoid criticism. This will not work, especially if we have any public role. It is true that the Bible says that we are to let our light shine that men might see our good deeds and give glory to God (Matt. 5:16). And it is true that we are to silence the ignorance of foolish men by our good deeds (1 Pet. 2:15). But there is also the truth that the world called the most loving Master of the house Beelzebul (Matt. 10:25).

You cannot be kind enough and merciful enough that no one will criticize you. For example, whatever one may think of the spirituality or theology of Mother Teresa (1910-1997), it takes one's breath away to hear feminist Germain Greer criticize her by saying she is a "religious imperialist."

At my convent school, the pious nuns who always spoke softly and inclined their heads with a small, patient smile

---

[58] Stonehouse, *J. Gresham Machen*, p. 375.
[59] Ibid., p. 387.
[60] Ibid., p. 413.

were the ones to fear. They became the mother superiors. Mother Teresa is not content with running a convent; she runs an order of Mother Teresa clones, which operates world-wide. In anyone less holy, this would be seen as an obscene ego trip. . . . Mother Teresa epitomizes for me the blinkered charitableness upon which we pride ourselves and for which we expect reward in this world and the next. There is very little on earth that I hate more than I hate that.[61]

In other words, let us forsake all notions that a life devoted to compassion will be spared criticism.

8. His early death at the age of fifty-five reminds us to find the pace to finish the race.

God is sovereign and works all our foolishness together for his glory. But our duty and biblical responsibility is to work in such a way as not to allow less important demands of the present to steal our strength—and our life—that might serve some greater demand in the years to come. It is hard to believe that Machen made a wise decision to go to North Dakota in the Christmas break of 1936-37, when he was "deadly tired" and needed rest so badly. It is also a rebuke that he was about thirty pounds overweight.[62]

Charles Spurgeon, the London pastor in the nineteenth century, had his own struggles with pace and health. He died at the age of fifty-seven. But he gives wonderful counsel to those who are prone to neglect the body for the sake of mental labor:

---

[61] Quoted in *First Things* (January 1993), p. 65.
[62] He was 5' 8" tall and for most of his life weighed about 150 pounds. But in the last ten years he allowed himself to reach 180. Stonehouse, *J. Gresham Machen*, p. 506.

Sedentary habits have tendency to create despondency. . . . To sit long in one posture, poring over a book, or driving a quill, is in itself a taxing of nature; but add to this a badly ventilated chamber, a body which has long been without muscular exercise, and a heart burdened with many cares, and we have all the elements for preparing a seething cauldron of despair, especially in the months of fog. . . . He who forgets the humming of the bees among the heather, the cooing of the wood-pigeons in the forest, the song of birds in the woods, the rippling of rills among the rushes, the sighing of the wind among the pines, needs not wonder if his heart forgets to sing and his soul grows heavy. A day's breathing of fresh air upon the hills, or a few hours' ramble in the beech woods' umbrageous calm, would sweep the cobwebs out of the brain of scores of our toiling ministers who are not but half alive. A mouthful of sea air, or a stiff walk in the wind's face would not give grace to the soul, but it would yield oxygen to the body, which is next best.[63]

One lesson we should learn is to be accountable to a group of friends who will have the courage and the authority to tell us, if necessary, to work and eat more wisely. Machen was not accountable in this way. Ned Stonehouse, his fellow teacher at Westminster at the end, said, "There was no one of sufficient influence to constrain him to curtail his program to any significant degree."[64] Who knows what a great difference it would have made for the whole cause of Evangelicalism if Machen had lived and worked another twenty years?

9. Machen's approach to apologetics raises the question

---

[63] Charles Spurgeon, *Lectures to My Students* (Grand Rapids, MI: Zondervan, 1972), p. 158.
[64] Stonehouse, *J. Gresham Machen*, p. 506.

whether our labors for the sake of the lost should not only involve
direct attempts to present the gospel, but also indirect attempts
to remove obstacles in the culture that make faith more difficult.

Machen certainly saw the intellectual challenge of his day
and rose to meet it with his remarkable intellectual powers. He
saw that an intellectual cultural atmosphere uncongenial to the
categories of truth will make the spread of the gospel all the
harder. One of the most provocative aspects of Machen's thought
is his contention that apologetics involves preparing a culture
more congenial to the gospel.

> It is true that the decisive thing is the regenerative power
> of God. That can overcome all lack of preparation, and
> the absence of that makes even the best preparation use-
> less. but as a matter of fact God usually exerts that power
> in connection with certain prior conditions of the human
> mind, and it should be ours to create, so far as we can,
> with the help of God, those favorable conditions for the
> reception of the gospel. False ideas are the greatest obsta-
> cles to the reception of the gospel. We may preach with
> all the fervor of a reformer and yet succeed only in win-
> ning a straggler here and there, if we permit the whole col-
> lective thought of the nation or of the world to be
> controlled by ideas which, by the resistless force of logic,
> prevent Christianity from being regarded as anything
> more than a harmless delusion. Under such circum-
> stances, what God desires us to do is to destroy the obsta-
> cle at its root. . . . What is today a matter of academic
> speculation begins tomorrow to move armies and pull
> down empires. In that second stage, it has gone too far
> to be combated; the time to stop it was when it was still
> a matter of impassionate debate. So as Christians we
> should try to mould the thought of the world in such a

way as to make the acceptance of Christianity something more than a logical absurdity. . . . What more pressing duty than for those who have received the mighty experience of regeneration, who, therefore, do not, like the world, neglect that whole series of vitally relevant facts which is embraced in Christian experience—what more pressing duty than for these men to make themselves masters of the thought of the world in order to make it an instrument of truth instead of error?[65]

Is there biblical warrant for this goal in 1 Peter 2:15? "This is the will of God, that by doing good you should put to silence the ignorance of foolish people." We are to silence the ignorance of foolish people by our good deeds; that is, we are to stop the spread of falsehood by powerful evidence to the contrary. Or is there evidence for Machen's view in Ephesians 5:11? "Take no part in the unfruitful works of darkness, but instead expose them." Or should we find support in Matthew 5:14-16?

You are the light of the world. A city set on a hill cannot be hidden. Nor do people light a lamp and put it under a basket, but on a stand, and it gives light to all in the house. In the same way, let your light shine before others, so that they may see your good works and give glory to your Father who is in heaven.

Does this light and salt include spreading the preservative idea that there is truth and beauty and valid knowing? Or perhaps most plainly we should find support for Machen's view in 2 Corinthians 10:4-5. "The weapons of our warfare are not of the flesh but have divine power to destroy strongholds. We destroy arguments

---

[65] Machen, "Christianity and Culture," pp. 162-163.

and every lofty opinion raised against the knowledge of God, and take every thought captive to obey Christ."

Is Machen's Idea Backward?

In one sense this idea of transforming culture so that the gospel is more readily believed may sound backward. In world missions the gospel comes first before the culture is transformed. Only then, after the gospel is received, is there set in motion a culture-shaping power that in several generations may result in changing some worldview issues in the culture that make Christianity less foreign even to the nonbeliever so that there are fewer obstacles to overcome.

But this process is not a straight line to glory on earth (some saved → culture altered → more saved → culture more altered, etc.). The process seems to ebb and flow as generations come and go. Being born and living in that ebb and flow one must ask: is it a crucial ministry to engage in debate at foundational levels in order to slow the process of deterioration of gospel-friendly assumptions, and perhaps hasten the reestablishing of assumptions that would make Christianity objectively conceivable and thus more capable of embracing?

The New Testament is a first-generation document. It was not written into a situation where the gospel had been known and believed for centuries and where the culture may have been partially transformed, then had degenerated, and was now in need of another movement of transformation. But there is an analogy to this kind of cultural situation in the Old Testament. The people of God did indeed experience the ebb and flow of being changed by the Word of God, and then drifting away from it, and coming back. So we might see in some of the reforming actions of the Old Testament an analogy to what Machen meant by preparing the culture to make it more receptive to the truth of God. For example, one might think of the removal of the high places by the kings (2 Kings 18:4), or the putting away of foreign wives by the post-exilic Jews (Ezra 10:11).

Machen may have put too much hope in the intellectual power of the church to transform the mind-set of a nation and make evangelism easier. In his speaking of renaissance and revival coming together,[66] he may have put "renaissance" in too prominent a position. I only say this as a caution that others have seen too,[67] not as a final judgment. However, it may be that in our even more anti-intellectual world of the twenty-first century we would do well to listen to Machen here rather than criticize him.

10. Should we learn, indirectly from the story of Machen's life, that prayer must be foundational to the use of intellectual power?

I ask it as a question because I am perplexed. It is strange that Machen's friend and close associate, Ned Stonehouse, in five hundred pages of sympathetic *Memoir*, said nothing about Machen's prayer life. And in the complete twenty-four-page list of Machen's writings in *Pressing Toward the Mark: Essays Commemorating Fifty Years of the Orthodox Presbyterian Church*, I found no essay or book on the subject of prayer, though

---

[66] "Christianity and Culture," p. 200; *What is Christianity?*, p. 118; *What Is Faith?*, p. 18.

[67] George Marsden observes, "Regarding Common Sense philosophy: as I have argued elsewhere, I believe it led Machen to overestimate the prowess of rational argument and underestimate the importance of point of view. Nonetheless, I also think that it helped Machen recognize some trends that few other mainline Protestant thinkers seemed worried about at the time. . . . Probably he overestimated the degree to which the task of the church in the twentieth century should be an intellectual one. On the other hand, I am convinced that he was right that many of his Christian contemporaries were underestimating the intellectual crisis they faced." Marsden, "Understanding J. Gresham Machen," pp. 198-199.

there is a section on prayer in *The New Testament: An Introduction to Its Literature and History.*[68]

Nor is there any reference to his devotional life—meditating on the Word for his own encouragement and strength. Nor is there any reference to personal worship and rarely to corporate worship as a driving force in his life. It seems as though all was swallowed up in the intellectual defense of faith. One wonders whether some ground may have been lost by fighting instead of praying. Of course, he may have had a vital personal prayer life—hidden in accord with the words of the Lord, "When you pray, go into your room and shut the door and pray to your Father who is in secret" (Matthew 6:6).

But that in all his writings he would not take up that topic, and that Stonehouse would not consider it worthy of highlighting as one of the powerful nerve-centers of his life and thought, is disconcerting in view of Machen's being a biblically-saturated warrior for the Word that commands, "watch and pray" as the heart of the warfare. Whether from silence about his prayer life or absence of its centrality, let us learn that without vital prayer, the fruitfulness of our labors will be less and our spiritual vision will be impaired.

11. We learn that God uses men who are persistently flawed.

Machen seemed to have a personality that alienated people too easily. The committee that did not recommend him to the chair of apologetics at Princeton referred to his "temperamental idiosyncrasies."[69] He seems to have had "a flaring temper and a propensity to make strong remarks about individuals with whom he disagreed."[70]

---

[68] Machen, *The New Testament*, pp. 319-329.
[69] Stonehouse, *J. Gresham Machen: A Biographical Memoir*, p. 389.
[70] Marsden, "Understanding J. Gresham Machen," p. 186. See above, n. 23.

Francois de Fenelon, the seventeenth-century French bishop, spoke soberly and perceptively on the imperfections of the saints: "It should be remembered that even the best of people leave much to be desired, and we must not expect too much. . . . Do not allow yourself to turn away from people because of their imperfections. . . . I have found that God leaves, even in the most spiritual people, certain weaknesses which seem to be entirely out of place."[71]

12. We should learn from Machen the dangers of bringing blind spots with us from our cultural background.

Machen may have lived at a level of cultural wealth and comfort that made it hard for him to see and feel the painful side of being poor and living without the freedom and luxury to travel to Europe repeatedly and go to hotels in order to have quiet for writing. The privations and pressures of the urban poor were so far from Machen's experience that the issue of how to minister more immediately did not press him as hard as it might have others, and so left him perhaps to develop his apologetic in a world cut off in significant measure from the questions of how it relates to the poor and uneducated.

Again I say this with some hesitancy, because all of us are limited by the cultural level at which we live. We see only so many hurts and problems. There are a hundred blind spots for every clear insight. Machen did give significant thought to the whole issue of education for children,[72] whether or not he faced the complexities of how to tackle the problems of the cities.

[71] Quoted in Clay Sterrett, "Hanging Tough," *Faith and Renewal* 16 (January/February 1992), p. 21.
[72] His essay "The Necessity of the Christian School" is a politically engaged and culturally sensitive plea for the national benefit of such schools as well as the benefit to the advance of the gospel. Machen, *Selected Shorter Writings*, pp. 161-173.

Hope in God's Sovereignty Through
Human Shortcomings

The overarching lesson to be learned from Machen's mixture of weaknesses and strengths is that God reigns over his church and over the world in such a way that he weaves the weaknesses and the strengths of his people with infinite wisdom into a fabric history that displays the full range of his glories. His all-inclusive plan is always more hopeful than we think in the darkest hours of history, and it is always more intermixed with human sin and weakness than we can see in its brightest hours. This means that we should renounce all triumphalism in the bright seasons and renounce all despair in the dark seasons.

When all seems to be going our way we should hear the words of James 4:14-15, "You do not know what tomorrow will bring. What is your life? For you are a mist that appears for a little time and then vanishes. Instead you ought to say, 'If the Lord wills, we will live and do this or that.'" And when all seems to be going against us, we should hear the words of 1 Corinthians 15:58, "Be steadfast, immovable, always abounding in the work of the Lord, knowing that in the Lord your labor is not in vain."

Both these extremes he avoided; he was sublime in action, lowly in mind; inaccessible in virtue, most accessible in intercourse; gentle, free from anger, sympathetic, sweet in words, sweeter in disposition; angelic in appearance, more angelic in mind; calm in rebuke, persuasive in praise, without spoiling the good effect of either by excess, but rebuking with the tenderness of a father, praising with the dignity of a ruler, his tenderness was not dissipated, nor his severity sour; for the one was reasonable, the other prudent, and both truly wise; his disposition sufficed for the training of his spiritual children, with very little need of words; his words with very little need of the rod, and his moderate use of the rod with still less for the knife.

GREGORY OF NAZIANZUS, ORATION 21:
ON ATHANASIUS OF ALEXANDRIA,
IN GREGORY NAZIANZUS, SELECT ORATIONS,
SERMONS, LETTERS; DOGMATIC TREATISES,
NICENE AND POST-NICENE FATHERS, 2nd SERIES,
ED. P. SHAFF AND H. WACE, VOL. VII,
PP. 271-272, PARAGRAPH 9

CONCLUSION

Contending for Our All:
A Golden Opportunity for Love

Contending for our all cannot be done in a way that contradicts the character of our all—namely, Jesus Christ. This means that when we contend for the fullness of Christ with our lips, we must confirm the love of Christ with our lives. All three of our swans knew this and labored to practice it.

How Athanasius "Snatched the Whole World from the Jaws of Satan"

Athanasius did not gloat over his emerging triumph in the doctrinal battle for the deity of Christ. He had not loved controversy. Victory was not his first delight. The worship of the divine Christ by the unified people of Christ was Athanasius's great joy. Not long after Athanasius died, Gregory of Nazianzus described how merciful Athanasius was with those who had opposed him. On his return to Alexandria from the third exile, he enjoyed the full authority of a beloved bishop. Nevertheless, "those who had been wronged he set free from oppression, making no distinction as to whether they were of his own or of the opposite party. . . . He treated so mildly and gently those who had injured him, that even they themselves, if I may say so, did not find his restoration distasteful."[1]

As the tide turned his way, Athanasius aimed at reconciliation, not retaliation. In the months of peace (February 362-October 23, 362) before his final brief exiles, he called a crucial council in Alexandria. The conciliatory spirit of this council was decisive in its redemptive effect on the entire movement toward orthodoxy.

> The importance of the Council is out of all proportion either to the number of bishops who took part in it or to the scale of its documentary records. Jerome (*adv. Lucif.* 20) goes so far as to say that by its judicious conciliation it 'snatched the whole world from the jaws of Satan.' . . . He saw that victory was not to be won by smiting men who were ready for peace, that the cause of Christ was not to be furthered by breaking the bruised reed and quenching the smoking flax. . . . The Council then is justly recognized as the crown of the career of Athanasius, for its resolutions and its Letter unmistakably proceed from him alone, and none but he could have tempered the fiery zeal of the confessors and taught them to distinguish friend from foe.[2]

All over the Empire the exiles were returning, and councils were being held repudiating Arianism and affirming the orthodoxy of Nicaea. Archibald Robertson tells us that these councils followed the lead of Athanasius in dealing with those who had formerly compromised themselves with Arianism. The love that

---

[1] Gregory of Nazianzus, *Oration 21: On Athanasius of Alexandria*, in Gregory Nazianzus, *Select Orations, Sermons, Letters; Dogmatic Treatises*, in *Nicene and Post-Nicene Fathers* [NPNF], Vol. 7, 2nd Series, ed. Philip Shaff and Henry Wace (reprint: Grand Rapids, MI: Eerdmans, 1955), p. 278 ¶¶30-31.

[2] *Athanasius: Select Works and Letters*, in NPNF, Vol. 4, ed. Philip Schaff and Henry Wace (1892; reprint: Peabody, MA: Hendricksen, 1999), p. lviii.

Athanasius showed in this controversy had the effect of "obviating countless schisms and attaching to the Church many who might otherwise have been driven back into Arianism."[3]

Owen's Remedy for Farther Evils That Come from Disputes

Similarly, John Owen knew that in contending for our all, the path of love must not be forsaken. But he made a crucial distinction between backing down from conviction, on the one hand, and loving the adversary, on the other:

> I can freely say, that I know not that man in England who is willing to go farther in forbearance, love, and communion with all that fear God and hold the foundation, than I am; but that this is to be done upon other grounds, principles, and ways, by other means and expedients, than by a condescension from the exactness of the least apex of gospel truth, or by an accommodation of doctrines by loose and general terms, I have elsewhere sufficiently declared. Let no man deceive you with vain pretences; hold fast the truth as it is in Jesus, part not with one iota, and contend for it when called thereunto.[4]

For Owen the discipline to kill his own sin[5] in the midst of controversy, and to pursue radical, personal holiness while "contending for his all," and to commune with God in the very truths for which he fought,[6] made love essential to controversy. In fact he

---

[3] Ibid., p. lix.
[4] John Owen, *The Mystery of the Gospel Vindicated and Socinianism Examined*, in *The Works of John Owen*, ed. William Goold (Edinburgh: Banner of Truth, 1965), X:49.
[5] See above Chapter 2, n. 40.
[6] See above Chapter 2, n. 75.

wrote a book titled *Evangelical Love, Church Peace, and Unity*. He admitted there that

> it is granted that they [the visible church] may fall into divisions, and schisms, and mutual exasperations among themselves, through the remainders of darkness in their minds and the infirmity of the flesh, Romans 14:3 ["Let not the one who eats despise the one who abstains, and let not the one who abstains pass judgment on the one who eats, for God has welcomed him"]; and in such cases mutual judgings and despisings are apt to ensue, and that to the prejudice and great disadvantage of that common faith which they do profess.[7]

But even though he granted that such "divisions and differences are . . . unavoidable," yet the "remedy of farther evils proceeding from them is plainly and frequently expressed in Scripture. It is love, meekness, forbearance, bowels of compassion."[8] Therefore he made it his aim to deal in his many controversies "without anger, bitterness, clamor, evil speaking, or any other thing that may be irregular in ourselves or give just cause of offence unto others."[9]

Machen on Christian Courage and the Heresy Hunt for Sin in Our Own Soul

J. Gresham Machen did not talk much about the condition of the heart in controversy. He was not given to describing the states of his own soul. His passion—and it was a great passion—was

[7] John Owen, *Evangelical Love, Church Peace, and Unity*, Works, XV:80.
[8] Ibid.
[9] Ibid., p. 81.

to restore objectivity to the Christian faith.[10] This had an interesting effect on his thought about virtue in controversy: he saw it in reverse. That is, he saw that courage in controversy is the test of a contrite heart. It works both ways. He said, "A man cannot successfully go heresy-hunting against the sin in his own life if he is willing to deny his Lord in the presence of the enemies outside." In other words, Machen saw the chief shortcoming of controversy not in the lack of humble love in the heart, but in the lack of humble courage in debate. Modernists were betraying their Lord while protesting their love. Therefore Machen made public confession the test of private love, not vice versa. "The two battles are intimately connected. A man cannot fight successfully in one unless he fights also in the other."[11]

Nevertheless he was explicit in speaking of his own aim to debate by the golden rule of Jesus. "I believe in controversy. But in controversy I do try to observe the Golden Rule; I do try to do unto others as I would have others do unto me. And the kind of controversy that pleases me in an opponent is a controversy that is altogether frank."[12]

Francis Schaeffer: Sweet-Singing Twentieth-Century Swan

One of the swans who sang most sweetly in the twentieth century was Francis Schaeffer (1912-1984), the founder of L'Abri Fellowship. He was a wise and humble apologist for the Christian

---

[10] "In *What is Faith?*, 1925, I tried to combat the anti-intellectualism of the Modernist church— the false separation which is set up between faith and knowledge." J. Gresham Machen, "Christianity in Conflict," in *J. Gresham Machen: Selected Shorter Writings*, ed. D. G. Hart (Phillipsburg, NJ: P&R, 2004), p. 564.

[11] J. Gresham Machen, "Christian Scholarship and Evangelism," in ibid., p. 147.

[12] Ibid., p. 149.

faith, and a model for many of us. In 1970 he wrote an essay called *The Mark of the Christian*. The mark, of course, is love. He based the essay on John 13:34-35 where Jesus said, "A new commandment I give to you, that you love one another: just as I have loved you, you also are to love one another. By this all people will know that you are my disciples, if you have love for one another."

Schaeffer spent most of this essay exhorting the church to disagree, when it must, lovingly. Schaeffer's view of biblical truth, like the swans in this book, was so high that he would not let the value of truth be minimized in the name of a unity that was not truth-based. Therefore, he dealt realistically with two biblical demands: the demand for purity and holiness on the one hand and the demand for visible love and unity on the other hand.

> The Christian really has a double task. He has to practice both God's holiness and God's love. The Christian is to exhibit that God exists as the infinite-personal God; and then he is to exhibit simultaneously God's character of holiness and love. Not His holiness without His love: this is only harshness. Not His love without His holiness: that is only compromise. Anything that an individual Christian or Christian group does that fails to show the simultaneous balance of the holiness of God and the love of God presents to a watching world not a demonstration of the God who exists but a caricature of the God who exists.[13]

Schaeffer knew that, in general, the necessary controversies and differences among Christians would not be understood by the watching world.

---

[13] Francis Schaeffer, *The Mark of Love*, in *The Complete Works of Francis Schaeffer*, Vol. 4, *A Christian View of the Church* (Wheaton, IL: Crossway Books, 1982), pp. 193-194.

You cannot expect the world to understand doctrinal differences, especially in our day when the existence of truth and absolutes are considered unthinkable even as concepts.

We cannot expect the world to understand that on the basis of the holiness of God we are having a different kind of difference, because we are dealing with God's absolutes.[14]

This is why observable love becomes so crucial.

Before a watching world, an observable love in the midst of difference will show a difference between Christians' differences and other people's differences. The world may not understand what the Christians are disagreeing about, but they will very quickly understand the difference of our differences from the world's differences if they see us having our differences in an open and observable love on a practical level.[15]

Therefore, Schaeffer called controversy among Christians "our golden opportunity" before a watching world. In other words, the aim of love, in view of God's truth and holiness, is not to avoid controversy, but to carry it through with observable practical love between the disagreeing groups. This is our golden opportunity.

As a matter of fact, we have a greater possibility of showing what Jesus is speaking about here, in the midst of our differences, than we do if we are not differing. Obviously we ought not to go out looking for differences among

---

[14]Ibid., p. 201.
[15]Ibid.

Christians; there are enough without looking for more. But even so, it is in the midst of a difference that we have *our golden opportunity.* When everything is going well and we are all standing around in a nice little circle, there is not much to be seen by the world. But when we come to the place where there is a real difference, and we exhibit uncompromised principles but at the same time observable love, then there is something that the world can see, something they can use to judge that these really are Christians, and that Jesus has indeed been sent by the Father.[16]

The Final Victory Belongs to the Lord

The heart-wrenching truth of our day, and every day, is that Christians not only disagree with the world about the fundamental meaning of life, but also with each other about serious matters. Therefore, we rejoice that it is God himself who will fulfill his plan for the church: "My counsel shall stand, and I will accomplish all my purpose" (Isaiah 46:10). We take heart that, in spite of all our blind spots and bungling and disobedience, God will triumph in the earth: "All the ends of the earth shall remember and turn to the LORD, and all the families of the nations shall worship before you. For kingship belongs to the LORD, and he rules over the nations" (Psalm 22:27-28).

Longing for the Day of Unity in the Truth

Yet one of the groanings of this fallen age is controversy, and most painful of all, controversy with brothers and sisters in Christ.

[16] Ibid., pp. 201-202, emphasis added.

We resonate with the apostle Paul—our joy would be full if we could all be "of the same mind, having the same love, being in full accord and of one mind" (Philippians 2:2). But for all his love of harmony and unity and peace, it is remarkable how many of Paul's letters were written to correct fellow Christians. One thinks of 1 Corinthians. It begins with Paul's thanks (1:4) and ends with his love (16:24). But between those verses he labors to set the Corinthians straight in their thinking and behavior.[17]

The assumption of the entire New Testament is that we should strive for peace. Peace and unity in the body of Christ are exceedingly precious. "Behold, how good and pleasant it is when brothers [and sisters] dwell in unity" (Psalm 133:1)! "Seek peace and pursue it" (1 Peter 3:11). "Let us then pursue what makes for peace and for mutual upbuilding" (Romans 14:19). But just as clear is that we are to pursue peace by striving to come to agreement in the truth. "The wisdom from above is first pure, then peaceable" (James 3:17). It is *first* pure. Peace is not a first thing. It is derivative. It comes from hearty agreement in truth.

For example, Paul tells us to set our minds on what is true, and honorable, and just; then the God of peace will be with us (Philippians 4:8-9). Peace is a wonderful by-product of heartfelt commitments to what is true and right. Hebrews speaks of the "peaceful fruit of righteousness" (12:11). Paul tells Timothy to "pursue *righteousness* . . . and peace" (2 Timothy 2:22). The unity we strive for in the church is a unity in knowledge and truth and

---

[17] He addresses the danger of boasting in leaders (1:10—3:23), the limits of sexual freedom (5:1-8), the extent of true separation (5:9-13), the proper handling of lawsuits (6:1-8), the goodness of sexual relations in marriages (7:1-16), the nature of Christian freedom (8:1-13), the proper demeanor for men and women in worship (11:2-16), how to behave at the Lord's Supper (11:17-34), the use of spiritual gifts (12—14), and the nature and the reality of the resurrection (15).

righteousness. We grow up into the one body "joined and held together" as we "attain to the unity of the faith and *of the knowledge of the Son of God*" (Ephesians 4:13, 16). "Grace and peace" are "multiplied" to us "*in the knowledge of God* and of Jesus our Lord" (2 Peter 1:2). And paradoxically, the weaponry with which we wage war for "the gospel of peace" begins with the belt of *truth* (Ephesians 6:14-15) and ends with the sword of the Spirit, the *Word of God* (v. 17).

Why True Unity Flows from Truth

The reason for this is that truth frees us from the control of Satan, the great deceiver and destroyer of unity: "you will know the truth, and the truth will set you free" (John 8:32; cf. 2 Timothy 2:24-26). Truth serves love, the bond of perfection. Paul prays for the Philippians that their "love may abound more and more, with knowledge and all discernment" (Philippians 1:9). Truth sanctifies, and so yields the righteousness whose fruit is peace: "Sanctify them in the truth; your word is truth" (John 17:17; cf. 2 Peter 1:3, 5, 12).

For the sake of unity and peace, therefore, Paul labors to set the churches straight on numerous issues—including quite a few that do not in themselves involve heresy. He does not exclude controversy from his pastoral writing. And he does not limit his engagement in controversy to first-order doctrines, where heresy threatens. He is like a parent to his churches. Parents do not correct and discipline their children only for felonies. Good parents long for their children to grow up into all the kindness and courtesy of mature adulthood. And since the fabric of truth is seamless,

Paul knows that letting minor strands go on unraveling can eventually rend the whole garment.

Thus Paul teaches that elders serve the church, on the one hand, by caring for the church without being pugnacious (1 Timothy 3:3, 5), and, on the other hand, by rebuking and correcting false teaching. "He must hold firm to the trustworthy word as taught, so that he may be able to give instruction in sound doctrine and also to rebuke those who contradict it" (Titus 1:9; cf. 1:13; 2:15; 1 Timothy 5:20). This is one of the main reasons we have the Scriptures: they are "profitable for teaching, for reproof, for correction, and for training in righteousness" (2 Timothy 3:16).

"By the Open Statement of the Truth We Commend Ourselves"

Faithful Christians do not love controversy; they love peace. They love their brothers and sisters who disagree with them. They long for a common mind for the cause of Christ. But they are bound by their conscience and by the Word of God, for this very reason, to try to persuade the church concerning the fullness of the truth and beauty of God's word.

We live in a day of politicized discourse that puts no premium on clear assertions. Many use language to conceal where they stand rather than to make clear where they stand. One reason this happens is that clear and open statements usually result in more criticism than ambiguous statements do. Vagueness will win more votes in a hostile atmosphere than forthrightness will.

But we want nothing to do with that attitude. Jesus refused

to converse with religious leaders who crafted their answers so as to conceal what they thought (Mark 11:33). Our aim (if not our achievement) is always to be like Paul when he said, "But we have renounced disgraceful, underhanded ways. We refuse to practice cunning or to tamper with God's word, but by the open statement of the truth we would commend ourselves to everyone's conscience in the sight of God" (2 Corinthians 4:2).[18]

This is the stance that the swans have always taken. This is the only stance worthy of those who are contending for their all—the truth of Jesus Christ.

[18] These final paragraphs are based on what I wrote earlier in John Piper and Wayne Grudem, "Charity, Clarity, and Hope," in *Recovering Biblical Manhood and Womanhood* (Wheaton, IL: Crossway Books, 1991), pp. 404-406.

Our Prayer
in a Time of Controversy

Gracious Father, have mercy on your children in disputes. We are sorry for any root of pride or fear of man or lack of insight that influences our stance in the controversy before us. We confess that we are not pure in ourselves. Even as we strive to persuade one another, we stand in need of a merciful Advocate. We are sinners. We are finite and fallible.

We take refuge in the glorious gospel of justification by faith alone through grace. We magnify Jesus Christ, our Savior and King, for all he has done to make us his own. We are a thankful people even in this conflict. We are broken and humble to think that we would be loved and forgiven and accepted by an infinitely holy God.

Forbid, O Lord, that our spirit in this struggle would be one of hostility or ill will toward anyone. Deliver us from every form of debate that departs from love or diminishes truth. Grant, Father, as Francis Schaeffer pleaded, that our disagreements would prove to be golden opportunities to show the world how to love—not by avoiding conflicts, but by how we act in them.

Show us, O God, the relationship between doctrine and devotion, between truth and tenderness, between biblical faithfulness and biblical unity, between standing on the truth and standing together. Let none of us be unteachable or beyond correction. May the outcome of our disputes be clearer vision of your glory and grace and truth and wisdom and power and knowledge.

By your Spirit, grant that the result of all our arguments be deeper humility, more dependence on mercy, sweeter fellowship with Jesus, stronger love in our common life, more radical obedience to the commands of our King, more authentic worship, and a greater readiness and eagerness to lay down our lives to finish the Great Commission.

In all this, Father, our passion is that you would be glorified through Jesus Christ. Amen.

♯⃟ desiringGod

Desiring God is a ministry that exists to spread a passion for the supremacy of God in all things for the joy of all peoples through Jesus Christ. We love to spread the truth that God is most glorified in us when we are most satisfied in him. John Piper receives no royalties from the books he writes—they are all reinvested into the ministry of Desiring God. It's all designed as part of our vision to spread this passion to others.

With that in mind, we invite you to visit the Desiring God website at desiringGod.org. You'll find twenty-five years' worth of free sermons by John Piper in manuscript, and hundreds in downloadable audio formats. In addition there are free articles and information about our upcoming conferences. An online store allows you to purchase audio albums, God-centered children's curricula, books and resources by Noël Piper, and over thirty books by John Piper. You can also find information about our radio ministry at desiringGodradio.org.

DG also has a whatever-you-can-afford policy, designed for individuals without discretionary funds. If you'd like more information about this policy, please contact us at the address or phone number below.

We exist to help you treasure Jesus Christ above all things. If we can serve you in any way, please let us know!

Desiring God
2601 East Franklin Avenue
Minneapolis, MN 55406-1103

Telephone: 1.888.346.4700
Fax: 612.338.4372
Email: mail@desiringGod.org
Web: desiringGod.org

INDEX OF SCRIPTURES

INDEX OF PERSONS

INDEX OF SUBJECTS